Shaam-e-Awadh

A Visual Journey of Lucknow

Shaam-e-Awadh

A Visual Journey of Lucknow

Vipul B. Varshney

BLOOMSBURY

NEW DELHI • LONDON • OXFORD • NEW YORK • SYDNEY

First Published, 2017

BLOOMSBURY PUBLISHING INDIA PVT. LTD.
New Delhi London Oxford New York Sydney

ISBN: 978-93-86432-44-5

10 9 8 7 6 5 4 3 2 1

Published by Bloomsbury Publishing India Pvt. Ltd.
DDA Complex LSC, Building No. 4, 2nd Floor
Pocket 6 & 7, Sector – C
Vasant Kunj, New Delhi 110070

Typeset by Fortune Graphics, Naraina, New Delhi

Printed and bound in India

About the Book

Shaam-e-Awadh – A Visual Journey of Lucknow, offers a visually arresting, storytelling and take on urban life from different perspective and artistic styles, as well as insight into various patterns of way of life in the old city and the newer parts.

Many facets of Lucknow are recorded here, as one strolls with sketchpad through gateways, courtyards and gardens, along broad streets and narrow alleyways, into great ceremonial buildings and cosy medieval chowks and nukkads. The splendour and grandeur of monuments are captured and enhanced with the beauty of the fauna and flaura of Lohia park. The ecsatsy of art of kiteflying is matched by the exotica of domes and minarets at the horizons of skyline of Lucknow. In few cities in the world, can such an array of architectural treasures be viewed within so compact an area, ideally suited to the visitor on foot. The mohallas and tolas of chowk to plush locales of embellished stone edifices of Gomtinagar, the book is a visual treat with the garnishing of historical anecdotes in the background. The beauty of wrinkled hands of chikanworkers and the pleasure of paan seekers are captured with equal deftness. The elegance of Kathak dancer's foot ghungroos to the mehak of phool wali galis are attempted to be reproduced in the form of...black and white sketches. The aroma of tundey kebabs of the dastarkwans are intermingling with the itrs of the bylanes produced by world famous perfumery. The Malihabaadi mangoes have no competition with the chaat of Hazratganj, yet both are an integral part of Lucknow as it seems. For every two pages, there's usually a description of the place or subject, and would usually have a historical background of the subject. There are the little bits of information that talks about the subjects, either the background of the buildings, or the food and people there. They are brief but interesting to read. It is a 135 page book, about A4 size. book features different aspect of Lucknow such as the architecture, art, culture, fashion, food, landscapes and people.

In order to make this legacy a part of every day experience, the INTACH Lucknow chapter propose *Shaam-e-Awadh – A Visual Journey of Lucknow*. This serves a dual purpose first to align the cognitive image of the city in the minds of citizen, tourists and city managers and second, to provide an armature for civic projects to improve the quality of the urban environment.

The specific objectives are to showcase the city to advantage to visitors; promote awareness about Lucknow's cultural heritage to generate concern among local people on wider issues of urban environment; inculcate/reinforce pride in the city's cultural heritage; highlight continuity between the past and the present to demonstrate that a city and its culture evolve organically.

Contents

Lucknow

The city of Nawabs, Kebabs and Tehzeeb!

The Golden City of the East

Lucknow,
the capital of Uttar Pradesh,
was historically known as the Awadh region. Fondly known as the 'City of Nawabs' or the 'City of Tehzeeb', it has always been a city filled with varied cultures. The city has been given various other names too: 'The Constantinople of India' and Shiraz-i-Hind. Lucknow offers, to its travellers, a unique combination of rich traditions and modern ways.

This is what makes Lucknow so endearing. A blend of simplicity and grandeur; rooted in history but not shy of taking modern strides. A city that has preserved its past and treasures its present. Emma Roberts who visited Lucknow in 1830 remarked, "In no other place in India can there be a more vivid realization of the visions of the splendid fictions of the Arabian Nights."

Times have changed but the name 'Lucknow' still brings passion to the hearts of several intellectuals and cultured people in many parts of India and even abroad. They say it has a class of its own that is far beyond the obvious. Its glorious past has blessed the city with a distinct character and a composite culture.

सुमित चाट भंडार

The Ancient Lucknow

PREHISTORIC TIMES

According to legend, Lakshmana, brother of King Ramachandra of Ayodhya (from which is derived the name of the region, Awadh), founded a settlement on a hillock on the southern bank of the river Gomti. It was named Lakshmanpuri after its founder.

EARLY HISTORIC TO MEDIEVAL TIMES

Somewhere between prehistoric and historic times, Awadh came to be controlled by the Bhar and Pansi tribes from the foothills of the Himalayas. Some families of these tribes, along with those of Brahmans and Kayasthas, lived in Lakshmanpuri. The earliest historical evidence of a settlement in what is now known as Lucknow is from medieval times.

At different periods starting from the 11th century A.D., it was controlled by various powers including the Saiyyids, the Khiljis, the Sharqis, the Pathans and the Shaikhs. The Shaikhs fortified the original settlement, which was called Lakhna Qila after its builder. According to one tradition, the name Lucknow is derived from this tale.

लक्ष्मण जी की नवनिर्मित प्रतिमा

The Legacy

THE GLORY OF LAXMANPURI

The ancient and early settlements of Lucknow were on the southern bank of the river Gomti, around Lakshman Tila. Underneath the Lakshman Tila, lie secured, fossilized ruins of 'Shesh Teerth' within the archaeological and cultural labyrinth of Lucknow. Till 1000 B.C, the pilgrims used to visit this great shrine to the west of the river, now known as 'Kudiya Ghat'.

MUGHAL TIMES

According to the famous historian Wheeler, Lucknow is one of the ten places where the Aryans came in ancient times. During the reign of Akbar was Shaikh Abdur Rahim, a fort near Lakshman Tila, known as Machhi Bhavan, because the twenty-six arches of the fort were decorated with pairs of fish. Shahganj's southern gateway is still standing, though in ruins, and is popularly called Akbari Darwaza. These buildings were bestowed on Mulla Nizamuddin by the Mughal Emperor Aurangzeb, who appointed him as one of the compilers of the Fatawa-i-Alamgiri at Farangi Mahal.

Lucknow has a glorious cultural past, where many buildings were built surpassing each other in beauty and splendour.

The sophisticated culture of Lucknow flourished from the last quarter of the 18th century until the collapse of the monarchy in 1856. However it continued to survive as long as the feudal system in this region, which was until the end of British rule in India.

During the 18th and 19th centuries, Lucknow witnessed unprecedented social and cultural development.

In view of the historical development of the city, the growth of Lucknow's architecture may be studied in three phases. Firstly, there are monuments dating to the Sur and Mughal eras, which have been completely neglected by art historians. The second phase of Lucknow's architecture spans the Nawabi era, i.e. 1775-1856. This phase has been further sub-divided into two, the first of which dates from 1775 to 1800, encompassing the reigns of Nawab Asafud-Daula and Nawab Saadat Ali Khan. While this phase witnessed exuberant building activity under the patronage of the two Nawabs, it is, architecturally, a traditional phase. On the one hand it represents the adaptation of later Mughal architecture, which was itself already in decline. On the other hand it was also the time when Claude Martin and the engineers of the East India Company were creating buildings In Lucknow.

THE TIMES OF NAWABS

The Nawabs of Awadh were indefatigable builders in their short span of eighty years. This phase is further divided into two phases. The first phase comprises those modeled after the Mughal style showing its degenerate transformed form; Bara Imambara, Asafi Mosque and Rumi Darwaza are regarded as the architectural glory of Lucknow. The second phase owes much to Nawab Saadat Ali Khan, one of the administrators and sagacious rulers of Awadh. His fascination for European architecture resulted in the erection of most of the buildings between Chhatar Manzil and Dilkusha, which include Lal Baradari, Kothi Farhad Baksh, etc. Most of these buildings are primarily influenced by the European style of La Martiniere constructed by Claude.

THE COLONIAL ERA

The British attached much significance to Lucknow, both for its strategic location and its socio-economic importance. The buildings of Colonial era of Lucknow, post 1857, are – Christ Church, erected within the Civil Lines; Cantonment Church, designed by Major Crommelin; Hussainabad Clock Tower, built in 1881, is the boldest architectural addition to Lucknow, designed by Richard Roskell.

While Asafud-Daula was building the magnificent Imambara Asafi, Martin was building palaces with European elements, which were to have a deep impact on the architecture of Lucknow.

Asafud-Daula's successor, Nawab Saadat Ali, was particularly enamoured of European lifestyle; he encouraged the construction of European buildings and took active interest in designing his own palaces.

The monuments of the second phase are characterized by a hybrid style, incorporating Indo-Muslim and European elements. The third phase comprises those monuments raised by the British between 1857 and 1947.The last phase is the Modern Era. The Modern era started with the appearance of Walter Burley Griffin (1876-1937) in Lucknow in November 1935, prior to Indian Independence. Griffin worked with his wife Marion Mahony Griffin and they brought a brilliant vision of modern architecture.

THE MODERN ERA

In India specially, commemoration or celebration of the memory of a leader, becomes a collective ongoing re-enactment in the public realm, something that the post-independence leaders exploited to their great political advantage. The very visible new five monumental projects in Lucknow include the Parivartan Chowk, the Prerna Kendra, Ambedkar Maidan, Ambedkar Memorial and Ramabai Maidan. Two of these are building complexes (Prerna Kendra and Ambedkar Memorial) and the remaining three are public spaces where the building structures are dwarfed by the extent of enclosed space.

Lucknow's most prestigious and big park, Dr. Ram Manohar Lohia Park, is approachable from this road. The park is devoted to Dr. Ram Manohar Lohia who was a great socialist and philosopher. It is spread over 80 acres of land. The clock tower is a major attraction of this place and The Lohia Path. Embedded in an 80-feet prism-shaped tower with sandstone cladding, the three specially designed clocks, at Rs. 5 lakh a piece, were ordered from the Johnsons of Kolkata. With Roman numerals, each clock has a diameter of around 4.5 feet.

QUALITY OF LIFE IT OFFERS

If Rumi Darwaza is the gateway to the Old City, the tastefully done Marine Drive now ushers you into Gomtinagar, often dubbed as modern Lucknow. The two constructions, though not in the same architectural league, together form our proud possessions. Elderly residents who spent hours in the greens of Begum Hazrat Mahal and Buddha parks in the past, now take strolls in Lohia Park. However, with changing times newer horizons have also emerged in Lucknow. Already a megacity of many splendours, the city today rubs shoulders with the best metros in India in terms of the quality of life it offers.

The Period of Wisdom

KUDIYA GHAT

Named after Rishi Kaundilya, the ghat was actually an ashram more than a hundred years ago. A Shiva temple stands testimony to the great history that lies silently in the backdrop. Rebuilt in 1990 and strategically set in a peaceful surrounding, the ghat has, in its vicinity, the age-old monuments of Lucknow like the Clock Tower, Rumi Darwaza and the world famous Imambara. The old iron bridge can be seen from this ghat.

SURAJ KUND OR SHAMSI TALAB

Suraj Kund, situated near the banks of river Gomti, is one of the sacred ancient places of Lucknow. It has been written in Ain-e-Akbari that "people from far-off places come here to bathe and worship." Abu Fazal has written that it is hardly 500 ft away from the Gomti. This pilgrimage has a tradition of holding a mela at its venue. Lucknow was supposed to be famous for Suraj Kund Mela.

This kund has five wells and a stone plaque which said that its centre has a particular point, which used to shine like the sun at noon, and was called 'Jyoti Kalash'. The wide and solid foundations

near the water tank hint at the presence of big settlements near the venue and a presence of a tunnel.

After understanding the significance of Suraj Kund and the mela, the fourth nawab of Awadh, Amjad Ali Shah, ordered an iron bridge to be constructed to facilitate commuting between the two areas.

This square pond was redeveloped along the old design in which there were bathing ghats on three sides except in the east where there was a slope for cows and cattle to drink water which came to be known as Gaughat. It was designed so that the person never has his back towards the east since the sun was supposed to be worshipped.

Suraj Kund: The main tank or the kund is a rectangular water body with stepped sides. It is located towards the east end of the park. There are several statues placed around the peripheral parts of the pond on pedestals. When the water level is high during the rainy seasons, the statues get partially submerged.

Surya Mandir: Towards the west of the kund is the famous Surya Temple. The temple has a square plan with a dome mounted on top of it using a short octagonal drum. The finial is an inverted lotus. There is stucco work on the base of the dome. The temple is seemingly built in recent times as there is no discernable historical typology of its architecture.

Navagrah Park: To the south of the pond is the Navagrah park which has plaques bearing the traditional astronomical information about the nine planets believed to influence human life. There are pathways and flower beds along the plaques.

Sundial: There is a metallic sundial to the south of the Surya temple, which is bordered on the west by steps arranged in an arc like a small seating of an amphitheatre.

People who used to suffer from skin diseases or eye-problems due to planetary positions were cured after the person took a bath in this kund. The cure is due to the presence of sulphur and other minerals in these water bodies. In the Mughal period, the Sheikhzades called it Shamsi Talab and therefore it was not damaged in that period. Even the Pathans respected its water. In the Nawabi era, the NawabAsafud-Daularejuvenated it by constructing new ghats.

Near this water tank is an old tree, underneath which the figurines of river Ganga and Jamuna are placed. These are believed to be the remains of some Math or temple, which were attacked by the invaders.

THE TILE-WALIMASJID

Tile-wali Masjid, also known as Alamgiri Mosque, is located to the north of the Imambara complex and is believed to be the earliest construction in the area. It is built on a mound specially raised by the order of Aurangzeb, governor of Lucknow, to serve as the mosque ground. An interesting fact is that "tile" is translated from the local dialect as "mound". Tile-wali Masjid is renowned for its outstanding architectural symmetry and equilibrium. Its white lace towers rise high and can be seen from most parts of the city. During the 1857 uprising, teachers and students of the madarsa fought for 80 days against the British troops, who had encircled the entire area. When the Britishers finally triumphed, except the mosque, they razed every building to the ground and hanged many freedomfighters on the tamarind tree just behind the mosque. For the next 50 years, the mosque remained in British possession but the Muslims were allowed to offer namaz.

NADAAN MAHAL OF MUGHAL ERA

The Mughals stabilized in Awadh during the reign of Akbar, and Lucknow became the seat of the subedar (governor) of one of the twelve provinces of the Mughal Empire. The first subedar, Shaikh Abdur Rahim, built a small fort near Lakhna Qila, called Machchhi Bhavan.

The tomb of Shaikh Abdur Rahim at Nadaan Mahal has a striking affinity with the architecture of Fatehpur Sikri. The significant use of Persian blue tiles can be seen on the dome and parapet of the buildings.

On the brackets which support the projection chajja, are seen forms of birds and elephants. Above the chajja runs the moulding, with two Cavettos and a broad central fillet. Maqbara Nadaan Mahal consists of two graves of saints who lived during the time of Akbar. This Maqbara is the only one of its kind in Lucknow. Tomb of Shaikh Ibrahim Chisti and a masjid can also be found on the premises of Maqbara.

AKBARI DARWAZA

Akbari Darwaza was constructed towards the end of Mughal emperor Akbar's reign by Gazi Mahmud of Bilgram, the Naib deputy of subedar (Governor) Jawahar Khan.

The erection of the lofty gateway was meant to honour emperor Akbar's visit to the city in the 16th year of his reign(1572), and for this reason it was named as Akbari gate.

During Mughal rule, criminals were hanged at the Akbari Darwaza for heinous crimes and their heads were severed off and thrown into the drain (Sarkata Nala). The gateway has rooms on both the sides and there are two jharokhas on either side of the arched gateways, used to spread flowers when an important person passed through it.

The gateway is in quite a dilapidated state with all the plaster peeling out and flaking. The gateway has also been encroached with various infrastructural facilities such as electrical wires, water pipelines and drainage pipes.

The Nawabi Era

MONUMENTS PAR EXCELLENCE

The Nawabs of Awadh

The beginnings of Nawabi rule in Awadh date from the second quarter of the 18th century. Sa'adat Khan, the first Nawab, was appointed Subedar of Awadh in 1732. He and his two successors, Safdar Jung (1739-1754) and Shuja-ud-daula (1754-1775), ruled from Faizabad and lived mainly there. They did not build anything significant in Lucknow, nor did they play any important role in its cultural life.

Shuja-ud-daula's son, Asafud-daula (1775-1797), shifted the capital from Faizabad to Lucknow, marking the beginning of the evolution of the city to its present form. This evolution started in the vicinity of Lakhna Qila and Machchhi Bhavan, and extended eastward along the river. The Asafi (Bada) Imambara complex, Roomi Darwaza, the Daulat Khana complex, all belong to this period. Roomi Darwaza today is virtually the signature of Lucknow.

Equally important is the advent of European influences during the latter part of this period, when the Residency and the buildings by Claude Martin and other European architects and engineers were begun.

Sa'adat Ali (1798-1814) was the next Nawab, whose reign saw a continuation and consolidation of the building activity and of the European influences. His successor, Ghazi-ud-din Haidar (1814-1827), was the first Nawab to be officially 'crowned'. The Nawabs now became titular monarchs, though only nominal rulers. Their allegiance shifted from the Mughal emperor in Delhi to the Governor General in Calcutta. The monarchy functioned under the supervision of the British Resident.

Muhammad Ali Shah (1837-42) was the next major builder among the Nawabs. His contributions to Lucknow include the Hussainabad or Chhota Imambara and the Jami Masjid. His buildings, integrating with Asafud-Daula's in an impressive scheme of urban design, brought a sense of a well-defined order to the Hussainabad area.

Wajid Ali Shah (crowned 1847) was the last Nawab, a prolific builder, a patron of poetry, music and dance, and himself an accomplished artist. To his reign belongs the Kaiserbagh complex of palaces and gardens and Sikandar Bagh. He was dethroned and deported to Calcutta after the annexation of Awadh by Lord Dalhousie. This was one of the sparks that ignited the uprising of 1857.

THE ELIXIR OF UNIQUENESS

Thus Lucknow developed its own identity not only in architecture but also in the decorative arts, music, poetry, theatre, dress, etiquette, hospitality, cuisine, and a number of other aspects of culture.

The Lakhnavi 'tehzeeb' and refinement of language, where even the rickshaw puller asks 'Kahan jaayenge, sahab?' (Where will you go, Sir?) is unmatched. Try calling someone 'tu' in Lucknow and just the resultant look of horror will suffice to make you mind your Ps and Qs for the rest of time. The world may only savour the Tundey Kebab with a fork and spoon, but inside Phoolon Waali Gali, brushing shoulders with cattle and man, the joy of sinking one's fingers into sizzling hot kebabs is reserved for the Lucknowite alone.

Asafi Masjid

The itinerary of a visitor to the 'bhulbhulaiya' of Lucknow is incomplete without a visit to the 'Masjid Asifi' with its well-proportioned domes and minarets. The mosque speaks volumes of the bygone glory of Nawab Asafud-Daula.

The most significant character of this building is its simplicity of architecture and proportionate setting of its constituents.

BADA IMAMBARA – THE MAKING OF CONSTANTINOPLE

It was the fourth Nawab of Awadh, Asafud-Daula who made Lucknow the permanent capital. He is also credited with its initial beautification and glorification. He was the first to build many beautiful palaces, gardens, religious and secular buildings of importance during his rule from 1775 to 1797.

Architectural Features

It took six years and nearly a crore of rupees to complete the extensive Imambara complex that was designed and planned by the architect Kifait-ullah from Delhi, then known as Shahjahanabad. The architecture in the Indo-Sarcenic style has a harmonious blend of Mughal and Rajput features.

The complex comprises two stepped gardens with tall gateways and a series of arched doorways (ghulam gardish) in the boundary. It has a big mosque known as the Asafi Masjid. Shia Muslims gather there to offer prayers every Friday and also hold the annual namaaz on the occasion of Eid and Bakri-eid.

Also known as the Bara Imambara, it is one of the architectural wonders of that era. Its central hall is said to be the largest vaulted chamber in the world. Except for the galleries in the interior, there is no woodwork in the entire structure. It has large underground passages which have been blocked. A staircase from outside leads to a series of labyrinths known as BhoolBhulaiya which is a complicated entanglement of zig-zag passages. Within the compound of the Imambara is the grand Asafi Mosque. Shahi Baoli is another attraction here.

THE BHOOL BHULAIYA

The Bada Imambara is said to be the world's largest arched room without any pillars.

The Bhool Bhulaiya in the building is three storeyed. It is surrounded with 489 doorless similar galleries, where one can roam endlessly for hours. This is why it is so mysterious. The structure contains various strategically built hollows in the corridors. There is also a blocked passageway which, according to legends, leads through a mile-long underground passage to a location near the Gomti river.

The Bhool Bhulaiya was constructed to confuse any enemy intruder. It is a labyrinth of hundreds of narrow stairway passages, some of which have dead-ends, some end at precipitous drops while others lead to entrance or exit points. The narrow lanes of the labyrinth can make anyone feel lost. The king and only a few others knew the way out. Simple in style, yet mysterious.

THE RITUALS OF MUHARRAM – ESSENTIALLY LUCKNOW

When Imam Hussain and Hasan, to safeguard their religion and tribe, were killed mercilessly at the battlefield of Karbala, mourning for the martyrs assumed great significance for the Muslims in general and Shias in particular. It is the Karbala tragedy which forms the pivot of Moharram, the basis for the manifestations of the unique and mass expression of grief and reverence toward Imam Hussain – not any less than towards Allah. This had led to the development of Imambaras or the place of Imam, not in any way meaner than the mosques, mainly meant for observing Moharram rituals, although during idle periods, it can be used for non-religious and social purposes also. One such example is the Imambaras built essentially to house the 'Tazia' or the replica of the tomb of Imam Hussain and to perform 'Matam'. Devout Shias donate food, as they come to hear, in their black mourning cloth, of the calamities faced by the martyrs of Imam Hussain and time stops for them as the 'Hadi Khwans', 'Vaquia Khwans' narrate the tales, and they, overcome with sorrow, weep again for them with renewed fervour. During the first ten days of the month of Muharram in the Islamic calendar, a variety of mourning rituals including majlis, matam, nauha khwani and soz is observed in the Imambara.

THE PICTURE GALLERY

Hussainabad Picture Gallery in Lucknow is situated near the Chhota Imambara and the Gallery Building is visible from the main road. It was built by the third Nawab of Awadh, Nawab Mohammad Ali Shah,in the year 1838 as a royal summer house. It is also called as Baradari as buildings made at that time were often called to signify 12 doorways.

There are around 30 stairs to reach the Picture Gallery. In front of the Picture Gallery, onecan view a large and beautiful water pond which enhances the charm of the Picture Gallery. Surrounded by green lawns and trees, it houses life-size portraits of all Nawabs of Awadh, which provides insight into the contemporary grand costumes and jewelry used by the Nawabs.

SATKHANDA

Built in 1842 by Nawab Mohammad Ali Shah, Satkhanda (now being renovated) looks like the Leaning Tower of Pisa in Italy. It is said that the Tower (67 metres tall) was built for viewing the moon by the clerics as Muslims celebrate their festivals according to the lunar calendar. Also, the Nawab wished this to have a bird's eye view of the royal buildings and the beautiful city of Lucknow. It could have been a most interesting building of the city and an important symbol of Awadh's past glory but because of the untimely death of the Nawab, the building could not be completed and out of the seven or nine floors, only four could be built by that time. There is an excellent blend of French and Italian architecture in the circular structure of Satkhanda. While the arches of the building represent Islamic architecture, Greek influence may also be seen in the four tiers of the structure.

CHOTA IMAMBARA – THE PALACE OF LIGHT

Though popularly called as the Chota Imambara, the Hussainabad Imambara stands to the west of Bara Imambara. Built by Nawab Mohammad Ali Shah (1837-42), it is more ornate in design with exquisite chandeliers, gilt-edged mirrors, silver mimbar and colourful stuccos adorning the interiors. A golden dome and fine calligraphy on the exterior of the building makes it a truly exceptional monument of Mughal architecture.

Chota Imambara is also sometimes referred to as 'The Palace of Light' in British history chronicles because of its decorations during the festive season. The gilded white dome and several turrets and minarets give this sparkling white structure a magnificent look.

The unique aspect of contrast is its golden dome and the fine calligraphy on the building exterior; its symmetry is seen on entering the central court; landscaping is based on the charbagh pattern. The hamam, on its entrance, includes a number of rooms finished in marble with depressed and raised baths, complete with provision for hot and cold water. Opposite the hamam is the Masjid turned toward the qibla axis. A lot of calligraphic designs have been used to decorate the façade. Generous elements of Persian crafts, the gilded white dome, and several turrets and minarets give this sparkling white structure a magnificent look.

THE ARTISTRY OF CALLIGRAPHY

The beautiful art of writing in Urdu, Persian and Arabic is known as Khushnavisi. The art of calligraphy or Khattati is derived from Khushnavisi. The decorative art of calligraphy dates back to the 12th century when masters in calligraphy came to India in groups. Kufi, nashkh, thulth, muhahhaq, riqa, diwani and nastaliq are popular styles of Islamic calligraphy.

It is believed that Mir Ali Tabrizi was the main propagator of this art in regions of Lucknow and Delhi. Nawab Sadaat Ali Khan also patronised this art during his reign. Hence, it was through writing in naskh and nastaliq that calligraphy reached Lucknow and attained a distinction that became unrivalled throughout India.

Various monuments in Lucknow are enriched with the art of calligraphy like the Chota Imambara, Karbala Talkatora, Imambara Zain-ul Abidin, Karbala Dayanat-ud Daula and Karbala Puttan Sahiba amongst others. In earlier times, people would decorate their homes with specimen of calligraphy. Calligraphy was very popular in medieval times and was used on coins, manuscripts, farmaans, books and other items.

CULTURE – THE TEHZEEB OF AWADH

The rise of Awadh, as we have seen, coincided with the decline of Mughal rule. Consequently, during the Nawabi period, the centre of patronage of art and culture in North India gradually shifted from Delhi to Lucknow. Delhi did retain its superiority of status but Lucknow offered more opportunity. Artists and master craftsmen flocked to the city. Catering to a different kind of clientele they adapted their skills to the new demands, which resulted in a distinctively different ethos.

This was reflected in the transformations which occurred in the established arts and crafts as well as in the new forms which emerged. When the sounds of tabla and tanpura hold an enthralled audience at Bhatkhande Music University, even the best-known names in the country give a standing ovation.

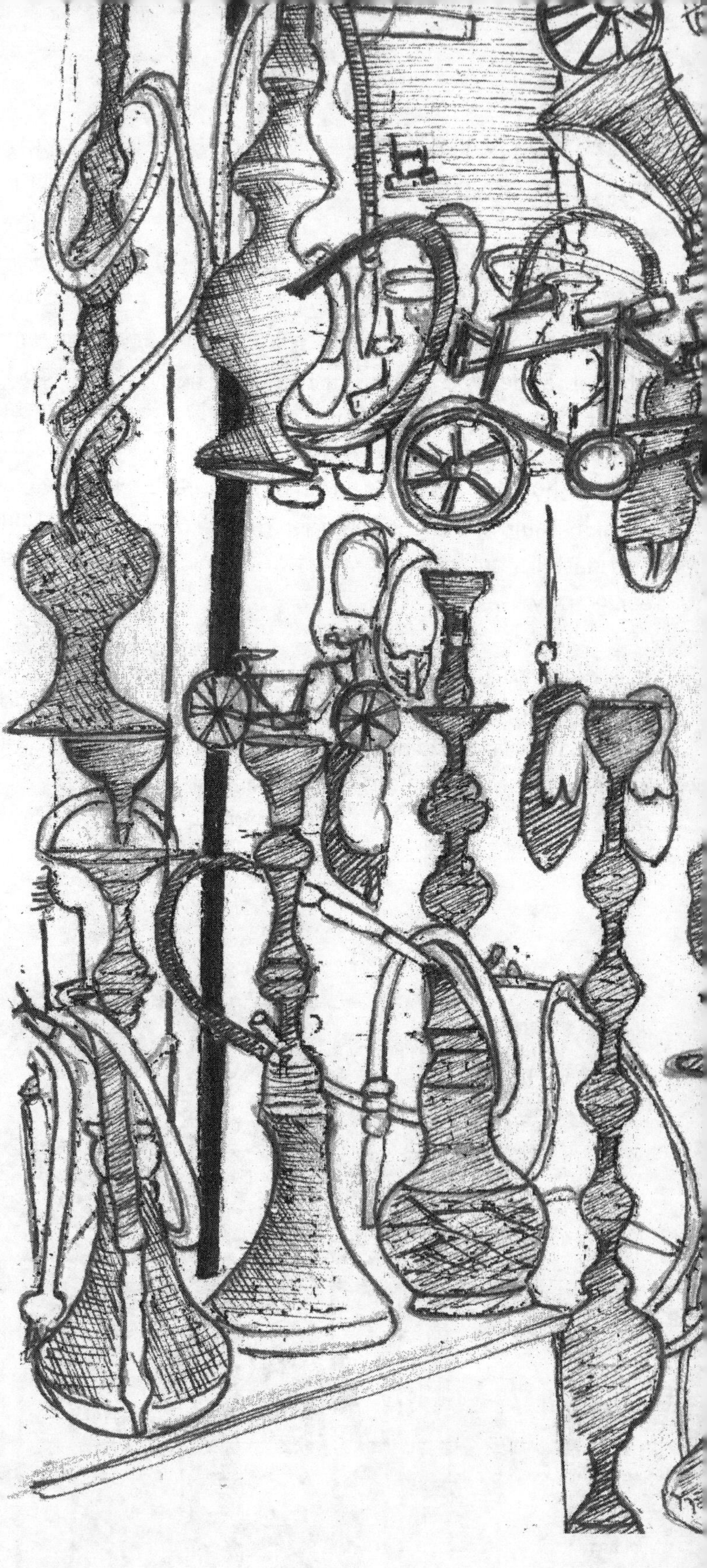

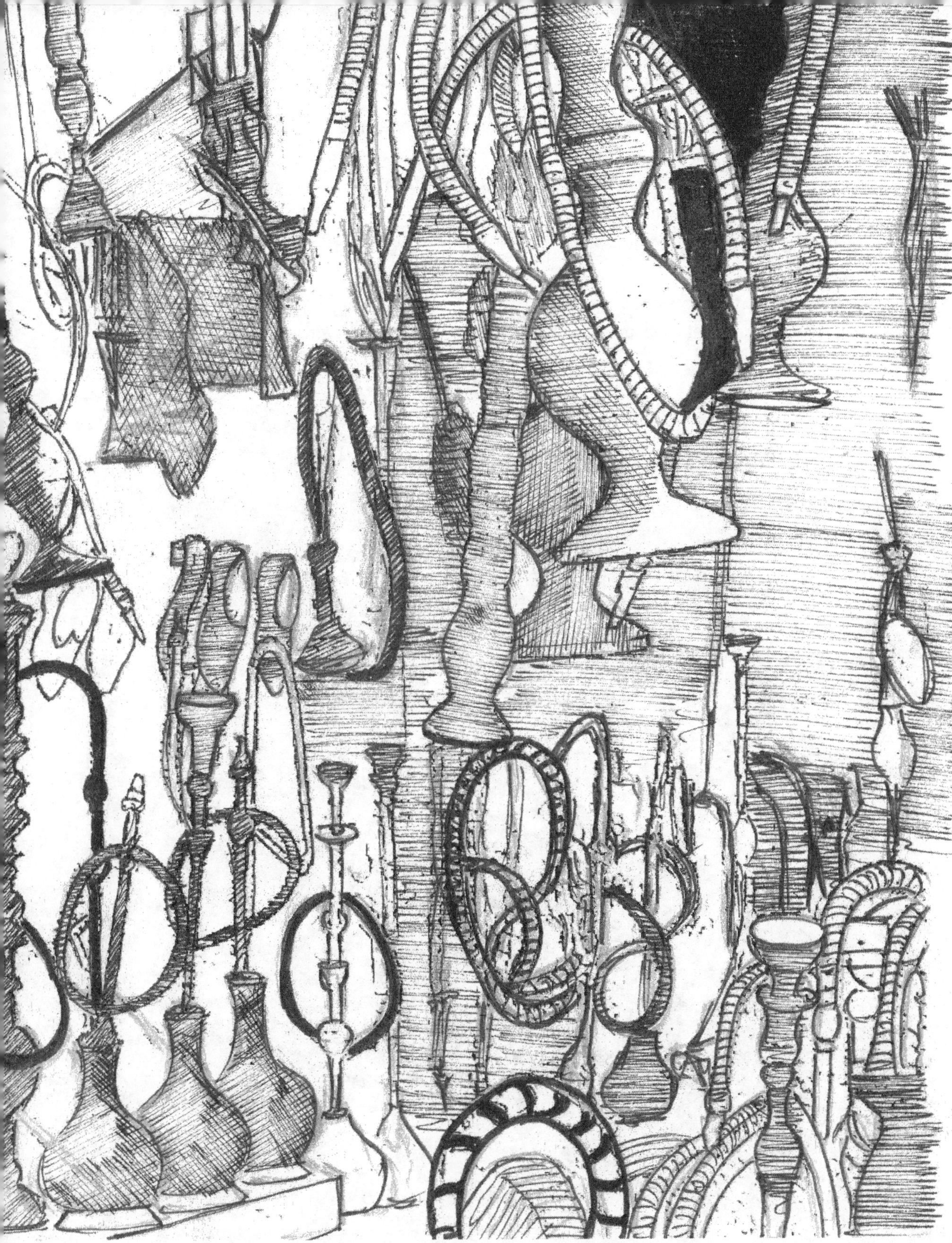

Whether it is the intricate web of chikankaari and zardozi or the steady 'thaap' of kathak of Pandit Birju Maharaj, the great exponent, Lucknow's cup of history is certainly brimming.

To assimilate the new into the old, to look to the present and the past for inspiration, is Lucknow's unique quality.

The attitude of people in the city is friendly and hospitable, unlike that in Delhi where people are pushy and commercial. There is an old-world charm about this place, which keeps bringing me back again and again.

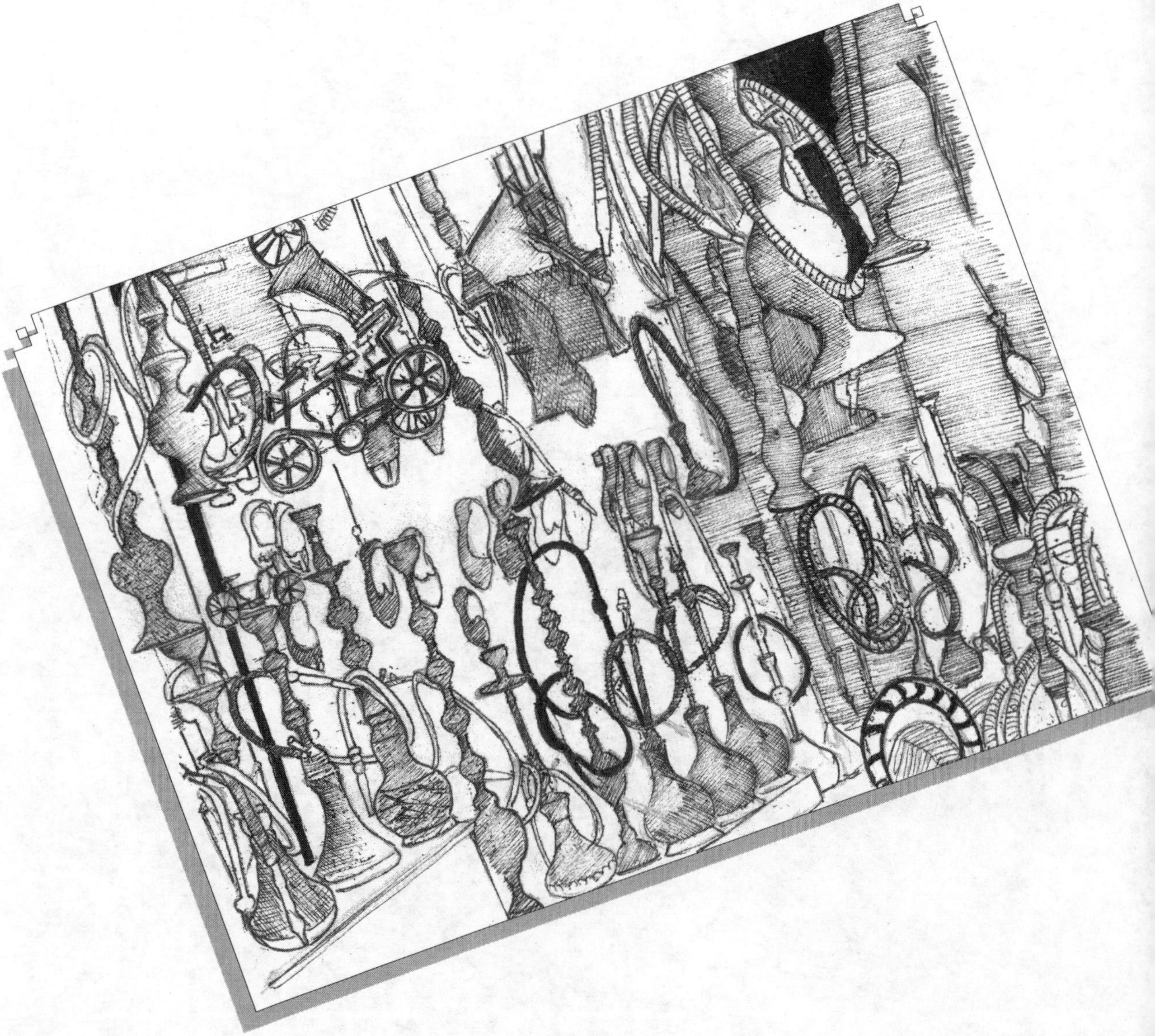

A TONGA RIDE IN THE OLD CITY

Tongas and tongawalas are integral to Lucknow's culture. It is said that the tongawalas of this city spoke impeccable Urdu, and had the aadab and tehzeeb a Lakhnavi would be proud of. That's why, in cultures that have been severed, people have lost their sense of beauty.

But here, the horse-drawn Ikka rubs shoulders with slick Audi Q6s. The 'galaoti' kebabs beat the chicken tikka masala hollow and capris embroidered with zardozi work are a routine affair in the narrow bylanes of Chowk. A walk through time-ravaged streets of Chowk is still a memorable experience because of the series of unfolding scenes – the rhythm of hammers beating silver into superfine paper called varq, the sweet smell of flowers, the fragrance of ittar (perfume), the intricate chikan embroidery and the mouthwatering aroma of roasting meat at a kebab shop. Not to forget the twitter of birds up for sale in the Nakkhas market. Venturing beyond the streets into the bylanes, you behold a private world of courtesans' houses with their many stories and anecdotes.

GRACEFUL TOMBS IN THE HEART OF THE CITY

The twin mausoleums were constructed with the characteristic lakhauri bricks and chunam. Embellished and decorated with delicate stucco mouldings and patterns, both the tombs are excellent specimens of Indo-Islamic style of architecture that was patronized by the rulers of Awadh after the decadence of the Mughal empire.

THE TOMB OF SAADAT ALI KHAN

Notsolofty in size yet renowned for its brilliant artistry, Maqbara of Saadat Ali Khan is onesuch famous landmark of the city. Situated near Begum Hazrat Mahal Park, this beautifully designed structure was built by Nawab Ghazi-ud-Din Haider and was meant to serve as a mausoleum for his father Nawab Saadat Ali Khan.

TOMB OF KHURSHEEDZADI

Placed diagonally across the mausoleum of Nawab Saadat Ali Khan, on the southeast, is the other mausoleum, that of his wife Khursheedzadi. Though the construction of this tomb had actually begun in the lifetime of Nawab Saadat Ali Khan soon after his wife's death, it could not be completed in his lifetime. The credit for completion of both tombs goes to Nawab Ghazi-ud-Din Haider.

Lakhauri bricks and locally available mortar was used to build this structure. Had this Maqbara been built with white marble, it would have transcended the beauty of the Taj Mahal. Just like Asifi Masjid, initially this Maqbara had rooms at the base of it. Later, they were closed permanently. The tomb of Nawab Saadat Ali Khan's wife Murshidzadi lies adjacent to his Maqbara.

THE MAGIC OF CHIKANKARI

A centre for the arts, Lucknow was where even alien art forms flourished to a high degree of refinement and amalgamated in its lifestyle as if these originated and flourished here itself.

'Chikan' style of embroidery is one such art that came from Persia but now is known with a prefix of Lucknow – 'Lucknow Chikan'.

Nawab Wajid Ali Shah, a great patron of art in all its forms, had 365 concubines. These so-called royal wives lived in Kaiserbagh and Chowk.As each lady got only a day to spend with the Nawab, they had to do something extraordinary to attract the attention of the king. One lady, to pass the boring hours in the harem, stitched a cap for the king and decorated it with simple but delicate white thread embroidery. This cap was later presented to the Nawab and the trick worked. Nawab started giving more attention to this queen and other queens followedsuit creating a creative pool of Chikankari in Lucknow.

Though the origin of Chikan work has not been affirmed, perhaps it is the corrupt form of the Persian word 'chikin' / 'chikeen' or 'sequin' which means a kind of cloth wrought with needlework. Amongst the many theories that go on to recognise the origin of this magnificent art the most believable is that it was brought by the Mughals from Persia and introduced through the Mughal courts into Dacca, East Bengal. Some say, Nur Jahan, the beautiful wife of Mughal emperor Jahangir, introduced chikan.

Chikan embroidery is today synonymous with the perfect lifestyle of Lucknow. The art has survived the ravages of time to stand tough and unique. Some artisans achieved perfection to the level that even a needle could not pass through the fine jaali work of Chikan. The grace that the Chikan garment promises is incomparable to any other dressing style; the simplicity, grace and comfort are the key words where Chikan of Lucknow is concerned.

ZARDOZI EMBROIDERY

Zardozi embroidery is the glitteringly ornate, encrusted gold threadwork practised in various parts of the country. An imperial craft brought to India by Delhi's first Turko-Afghan sultans in the 12th century, Zardozi became equally popular with the wealthy Hindus, Muslims and European elite down the ages. Today, several families in Varanasi, Agra, Lucknow, Rampur, Bareilly and Farukkabad specialize in this old craft and supply exquisite zari-embroidered bridal outfits and salwar kameezes to boutiques around the county. In recent years, Zardozi is also combined with Dabka work which is originally said to be from Lucknow.

Raw materials used are Metal Wire, Embellishments, Zari-Kalabattu, Tarkshi, Kasab, and in Zari Terminology-Gijai, Sitara, Salma-Sitara, Tikora, Kora chikna, Karchob, Thapa, etc.

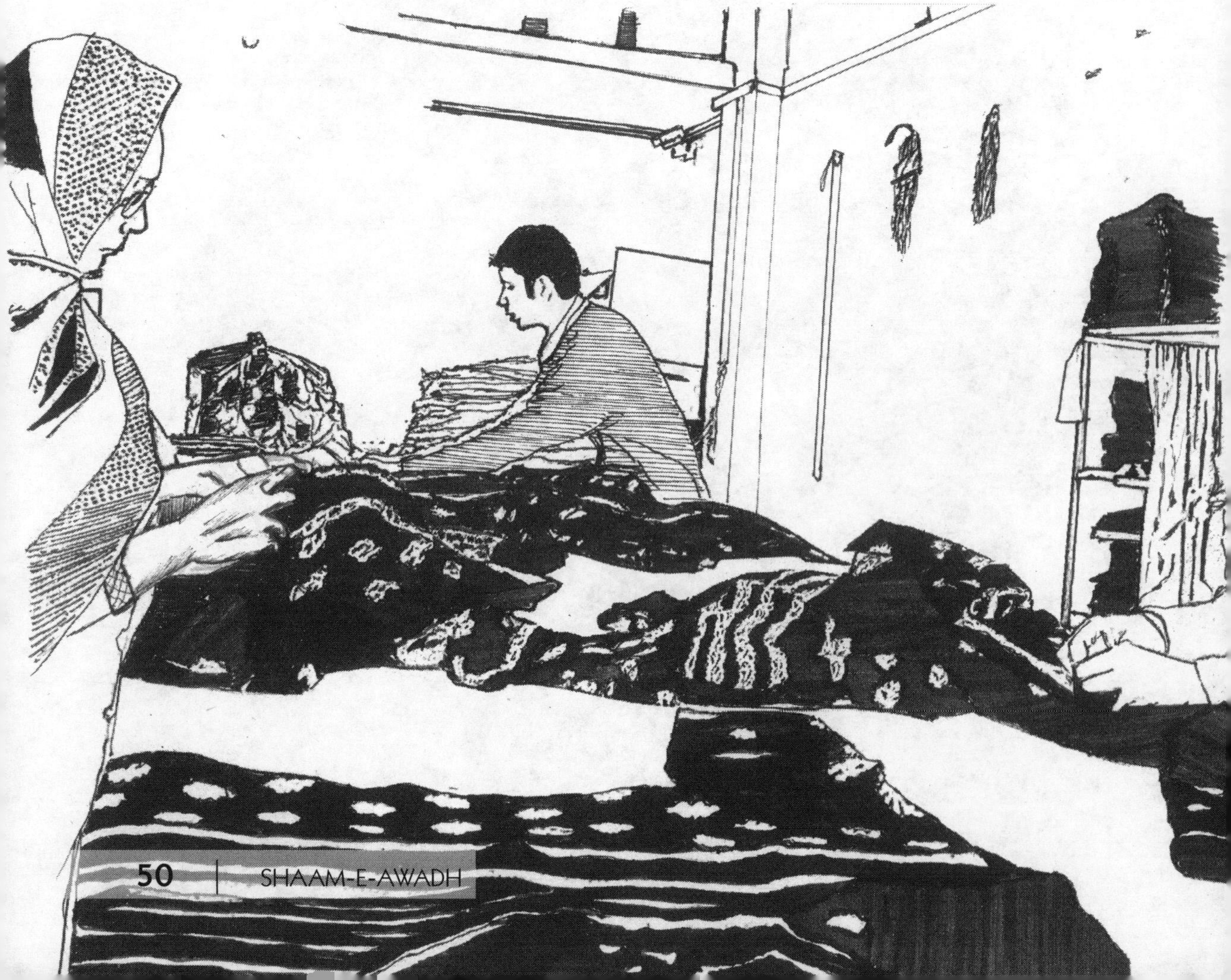

CULINARY ETIQUETTES

Culinary skills too reached the heights of excellence as the Nawabs were not only gracious hosts but also extremely fond of good, tasty and nutritious food. The art of slow cooking was perfected in Awadh. Utensils are made either of silver or copper. Kebabs are cooked in a Mahi Tava (large, round shallow pan), using a Kafgir which is a flat, long-handled ladle for turning Kebabs and Paranthas. Bone China plates and dishes were also used in Lucknow since the times of the Nawabs. Water was normally sipped from copper or silver tumblers and not glasses. The seating arrangement, while eating, was always on the floor where beautifully embroidered Dastarkhwans were spread on mats or carpets oreven Chandnis (white linen). Sometimes this arrangement was made on low-raised wooden tables called Takahts.

THE NEED FOR KABOOTARBAAZI IN AWADH

Kabootar Baazi was first introduced in Delhi during Mughal times and by degrees made its way to Lucknow where it gained popularity with the people. Kabootar Baazi tournaments are occasionally held in Lucknow in which teams from different parts of the state are invited to participate. After the Battle of Buxor between Lord Clive and Nawab Shuja-ud-daulah, there was no war in Awadh. As a result the people of the state started losing interest in martial arts and almost lost their martial ardour. In order to inculcate martial qualities in their subjects, the Nawabs of Awadh took keen interest in Kabootar Baazi, Bater Baazi, Murgh Baazi and Patang Baazi while their subjects followed suit. This psychological prescription proved to be effective and its results were fully manifested during our first war of independence.

THE TALKATORA KARBALA

It is well known in India and southwest Asia. During Muharram, Shiite devotees take their tazias to Talkatora, while Sunnis bury their tazias at Phool Katora, an area adjacent to it.

The tripolia (three-arched gateway) on the road to Rajajipuram serves as the main entrance to the Karbala. It faces the Imambara of Kaiwan Jah, which is ornamented with beautiful foliage and floral designs and borders of exquisite calligraphic inscriptions of Quranic verses, which are painted on the inside walls of its halls. Stucco mouldings embellish the arches and pillars of the two halls and shahnashin of the Imambara. The floral decoration and calligraphy is also there, in stucco, on the facade.

HUSSAINABAD CLOCK TOWER

It's truly the finest structure of British architecture in India.It was built by Hussainbad Endowment Trust in the year 1887 at a cost of 1.75 lakhs at that time, to mark the arrival of Sir George Cooper, who was the first Lt. Governor of Awadh. The design and map of this lofty tower was prepared by Roskell Payne and one can see the impact of Victorian-Gothic style on it. The width of the tower is 20 ft and height is 230 ft (67 meters).

Some parts of the clock are made of gunmetal and its components were imported from London. Its principal wheel is one and a half inches thick and has a diameter of 2 ft, which probably makes it larger than the Westminster clock.

THE SPLENDOUR OF HAZRAT GANJ

This splendid road was planned as a processional route by Saadat Ali Khan with two imposing ceremonial gateways, half Grecian & half Moorish at either end, to cordon off the exclusive Royal Residential Enclave from the rest of the settlements.

The area between the two gates was the royal residential area, where the Nawab's sons lived. The first gate might have been at the beginning of Hazratganj atthe General Post Office end, and the second gate beyond Kothi Noor Baksh, now the District Magistrate's residence. In between, on either side stood grand houses which Nawab Saadat Ali Khan is said to have built for his sons.

Hazratganj has undergone a number of name changes. Known in the British era as Queen's Way, it later became Janpath, and today, the portion from the Ashok Marg crossing to Tulsi Cinema is called Mahatma Gandhi Marg.

THE ELEGANCE OF GANJ

Lucknow is an incredible city, no doubt, but now it has an odd arrangement of buildings wherein the new and tall ones are pushing hard to squeeze into spaces sheltering old heritage buildings and monuments. Like the camel in the tent story, the old and infirm occupant will gradually be pushed out and forced to perish.

THE OLD-WORLD CHARM...

As the Mughal power in Delhi declined, the culture of its successor state Lucknow flourished, and artisans and artists, poets and musicians flocked to the city where the rich and powerful lived.

Lucknow has had its share of development; it is not fossilized, yet there is enough of visible history in stone, bricks and mortar, town planning, parks and artifacts, to stir the heart of the citizen and the imagination of the visitor.

NOSTALGIA OF GANJING

Many people assume that Hazratganj continues westwards along the old Strand Road, today's Mahatma Gandhi Road, but this is not so. Bishop Reginald Hebber, who visited Lucknow as early as 1824–1825, describes Hazratganj in 'Narrative of a Journey Through the Upper Provinces of India', published in 1829: 'Wider than the High Street at Oxford,but giving some distant resemblance to it in colour of its buildings and the general form of Gothic style of the greater part of them....'

Post independence, keeping in view the changed government entertainment policies, the Ballroom situated on the first floor was closed and the same premises were rented to the British Council Library. With an elegant reading room and a huge selection of books, the British Council Library became an overnight rage with the local intelligentsia. Downstairs, Kwality Restaurant, Ram Advani Booksellers and Mayfair Cinema Hall complemented one another! Alas no more!!

THE SPIRIT OF AWADHI LAND!!

Before converting into a cinema hall during the Raj era, Mayfair was a Ballroom patronized by the British and a select few Indian elite. With the exclusive Kwality Restaurant attached, it offered fine wining and dining to its patrons.

There is anonymity in big cities; people are unable to bond due to the hectic pace of life. On the contrary, the spirit of neighbourhood still lingers here. More the things change, more they stay the same. This forms the theme of Awadhi land, which has kept pace with the changing times without losing the pulse of the city.

GALLIS AND MOHALLAS OF LUCKNOW

Lucknow has its own world of streets and alleys which are famous for work done in them or for some other identity. For instance,some streets are based on caste names like Gujrati gali, Marwadi wali gali, Singhan ki gali, Kaysthon ki gali, Sunaron ki gali, Babbu wali gali, gali Narayan das, etc., whereas others are named after the businesses in them like Meena wali gali, Baan wali gali, Kanghi wali gali, Phool wali gali, Churi wali gali, Batashe wali gali, gali Hammam, Taar wali gali, Laiya wali gali, Chik wali gali, Patthar wali gali, Sirke wali gali, Taape wali gali, Sheermal wali gali, Dari wali gali, Joote wali gali, Janaab ki gali, Peepal wali gali, Chaawal wali gali, Parche wali gali, Maide wali gali, Gali meet mata, Kaale ki gali, Bhainse wali gali, Gadhe wali gali and Achhuti gali...

WINDING ALLEYS WITH GLORIOUS PAST

Master Amritlal Nagar used to call these alleys as 'Binoculars of Lucknow'. Revering Chowk's Baan wali gali as his workplace, Mr. Nagar used his brother Madanlal Nagar's painting for the cover of his novel ShatranjKeMohre, in 1957, in which Lucknow's alleys were distinctly portrayed. The Khinni wali gali had Mir Taqi Mir's Daulatkhana. Peenas wali gali has Maulwi Anwar Bagh abutted to it, where Hazrat Mohani Sahab was cremated. Taksaal wali gali is at Hiran Park Chauraha, where Hazrat Nasikh was buried. Mirza Dabeer was buried at Kucha-e-Dabeer, whereas the king of Mersiah, Mir Anees, was buried at Kucha-e-Mir Anees. The master of music Naushad resided in the alleys of Darsani Peer.

THE HUSTLE-BUSTLE OF AMINABAD

Nawab Asafud-Daula gave the area of Aminabad to Shah Alam-II in 1759 who constructed an Imambara, a Feelkhana (Elephant House) and a garden along with a number of shops. After his death, his wife sold the entire property to Imdad Hussain Khan Aminaddaula. Imdad Hussain added further constructions to the market that was then known as Aminabad.

Aminabad is the heart of Lucknow and the market is now165 years old. In the central area of Aminabad Market one may see a park of sorts, but with an underground parking. It is the historical Aminuddaila Park where the freedom fighters first hoisted the tricolour in 1928. Since then it is known as Jhandewala Park.

The blending of various cultural strains nurtured by centuries of Mughal and later Delhi Sultanate rule and the folk traditions of the Indo-Gangetic plains has produced a rich and complex mosaic of Indian culture. It was here that the Urdu language acquired its amazing phonetic nuances and refined suaveness. Lucknow has also cradled classical art forms like Kathak, Thumri and Dadra. Lucknow truly is a history lovers delight. It forms the link between tradition and modernity.

SHOPAHOLICS AT GADBADJHALA

Take an evening walk at Aminabad market and find some of its bustling bazaars that are so very exciting to shop at. Or for that matter Swadeshi Market that religiously stopped selling foreign goods when Mahatma Gandhi gave the call to shun foreign goods. Also Gadbadjhala, known for its highest bargaining shops, where one can get the prices reduced to 200% at times, if only one has the skills to bargain.

GANGA-JAMUNI

Lakhnau – the name itself signifies a culture that exudes warmth and an exquisite graciousness. While the symbiotic existence of various communities and the sublime old-world charm of Lucknow are precious to us, they are enigmatic and extraordinary to the global tourist who visits the city to experience these attributes that are part of the city's nafasat and mehmaan nawazi.

THE JOY OF FLEA MARKET

The markets are Mohan Market, Pratap Market, Gadbadjhala and Guin Road Stationery Market, Fruits market, Ganeshganj, Shri Ram Road, etc.

Three cinema halls still show movies. One can also enjoy tasty Desi Ghee Ki Kachauri at Kbra ke pas vali Dukan and Prakash ki Kulfi.

THE STORY BEHIND CULINARY EXCELLENCE!!

The cuisine of Lucknow at the time of the Nawabs was very much a cuisine of fusion. With the dual purpose of providing work (meaning food) and beautification of the city, Nawab Asafud-Daula commenced the building of the Bara Imambara during the great famine circa 1780.

Labourers worked during the day, and those of higher classes during the night, so their shame was shrouded. According to the menu at Dum Pukht: 'By royal decree, too, arrangements were made to provide food. Enormous containers were filled with rice, meat, vegetables, and spices and sealed. Hot charcoal was placed on top and fires lit underneath while slow cooking ensured that food was available day and night.'

The result was extraordinary, for when the vessels were unsealed, the splendid aromas attracted royal attention and Dum Pukht as a Nawabi cuisine was born. This is the case with the shir mal, also found in the gullies of the old city.

A.B.C CORNIR

HANUMAN TEMPLE – THE PECULIARLY SECULAR

Nawab Mohammad Ali Shah's Begum Rabiya established this temple in Lucknow. It is said that once she had a dream that there was a grand statue of Hanumanji lying near a garden and that she should dig it out and keep it in a temple. After she was blessed with a child, the Nawab immediately started excavating that place. To his utter surprise he found a statue of Hanumanji there. Nawab ordered that the statue be established in a temple near Bara Imambara. While the statue was being taken there, the elephant carrying it stopped and sat down at a place in Aliganj. A number of efforts to get the elephant up proved futile. On the advice of a saint of the area, Begum ordered that Hanumanji be established at the very spot.

TRADITION OF BADA MANGAL

The tradition of Bada Mangal has a history like this: Begum Janab-e Alia (wife of the third Nawab of Awadh, Shuja-ud Daulah – 1753-1775), dreamt of a divine presence commanding her to build a temple honouring Hanumanji. The dream pointed her to a specific site where an idol of Hanumanji was buried. The Begum inferred this as another divine sign and ordered the erection of a temple at this spot (Aliganj temple).

People from far-off places come to this temple to offer prayers to the lord. The famous festival of 'Bada Mangal' is associated with this ancient temple. It's celebrated grandly in this temple every year. An annual fair known as 'Bada Mangal ka Mela' is also held here at the same time.

DILKUSHA PALACE

The house was constructed around 1800 by the British resident Major Gore Ouseley,a friend of the ruler of Oudh, Nawab Saadat Ali Khan. It was initially intended as a hunting lodge for the nawabs of Oudh although it was later used as a summer resort too. Changes were made to its design by Nawab, King Nasir-ud-Din Haider (1827–1837). The Nawab only saw this building on its completion and the first words that came to his lips were "Dil khush hua" meaning "My heart is pleased", thus it was aptly named 'Dilkusha'.

It is said that in 1830, Dilkusha Kothi was the location for an early balloon ascent by an Englishman. This story is less notable given that the Frenchman Claude Martin had been a neighbour when his palace of Constantia, later La Martiniere Boys College, was started in the 1790s. He too had arranged a balloon ascent in Lucknow but he died before the demonstration could take place. The ascent in 1830 was watched by King Nasir-ud-Din Haider and a large number of his courtiers.

The sight of the ruins of lofty buildings built in 'Gothic Style' casting their long shadows on the natural carpet of lush green grass and beds of flowers is breathtaking.

DIL KHUSH HUAA

Stucco could be used to produce effects in deep relief even when applied to a flat wall with a variety of motifs ranging from floral designs, false arches and false domes, producing an exceptional surface articulation of walls, columns and ceilings. In using this technique, the artisans displayed exceptional technical skill, and the delicate execution of ornamental details and mouldings, consisting mostly of foliated and incised designs. The stucco ornamentation used in Lucknow was partly composed of mother-of-pearl and shells deposited in lake beds, and its shine was finer than that of marble.

LAMARTINIERE – THE GLORY OF GOTHIC FOLLY

LaMartiniere was originally known as Constantia. Historians say that this was from Martin's Motto 'Lahore et Constantia' (toil and fidelity) which is engraved over the first floor balcony. But romantic people believe it was named after Constance, who was Martin's first love, the young girl he left behind in France. In 1803 Lord Valencia visited Constantia and remarked, "It is a strange fantastical building of every species of architecture." In 1812 Lady Nugent wrote, "The house is intended to be in the style of an old French chateau, but it is a singular mixture of all sorts of styles; yet it is beautiful and interesting, as well as extraordinary."

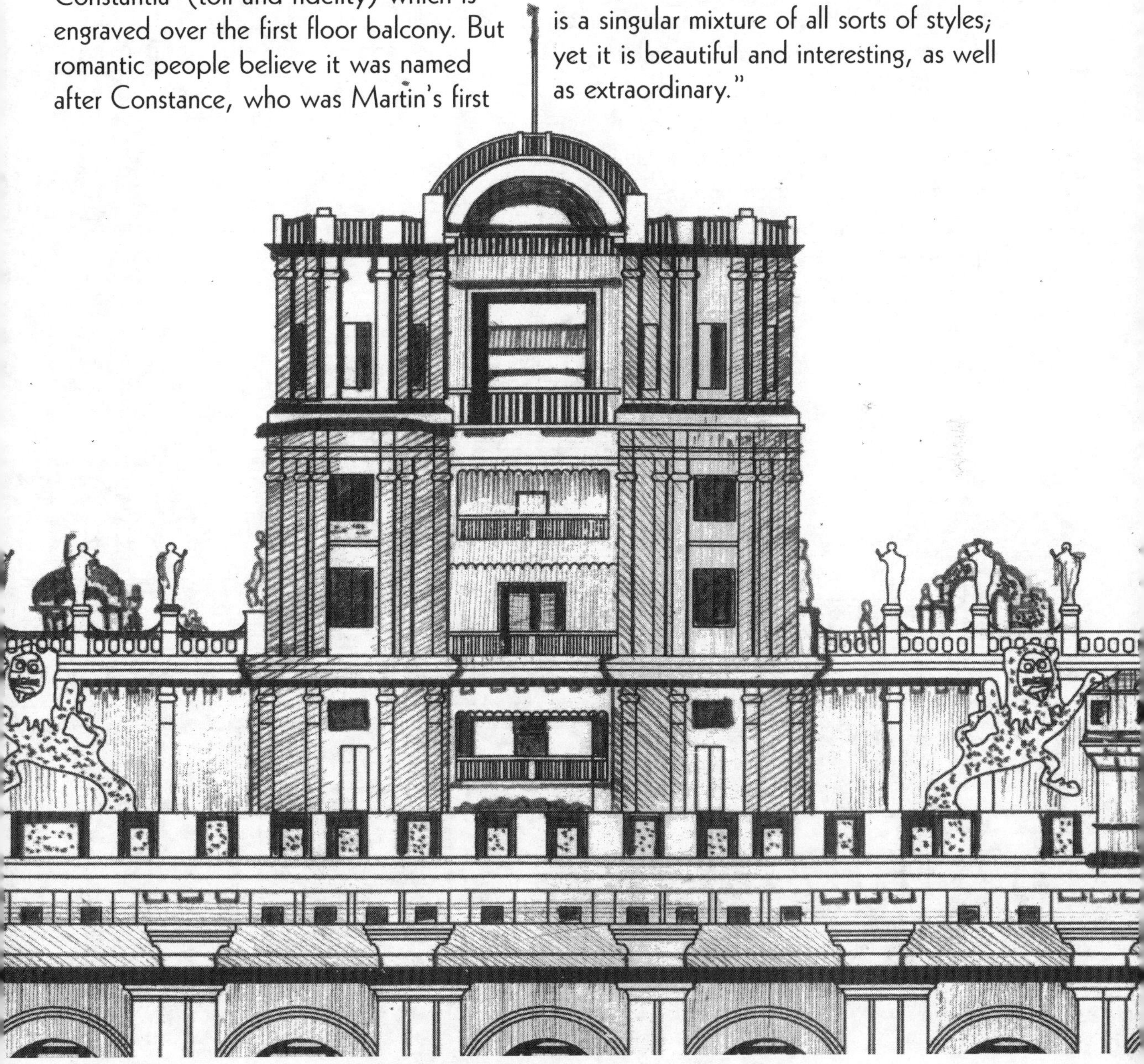

It has been described as a wedding cake in brick, a Gothic castle and a baroque folly. Four great octagonal towers, from basement to roof, form the framework of La Martiniere. Claude Martin designed his buildings like miniature forts, with cannons on the parapets and thick iron doors that sealed off spiral staircases and archways. There are 'secret' chambers on the first floor where cannon balls could be stored. The lion statues on the parapet were designed to hold flaming torches inside their open mouths. The sight of these illuminated beasts, belching out fire and smoke on a dark night must have been a terrifying one for would-be intruders.

The two cannons which stand on the terrace today are also a reminder of less peaceful days. One was actually cast by Martin in his Lucknow Arsenal, and named Cornwallis after the Governor-General. The other was captured at Seringapatam, when Martin accompanied Cornwallis as his aide-de-camp.

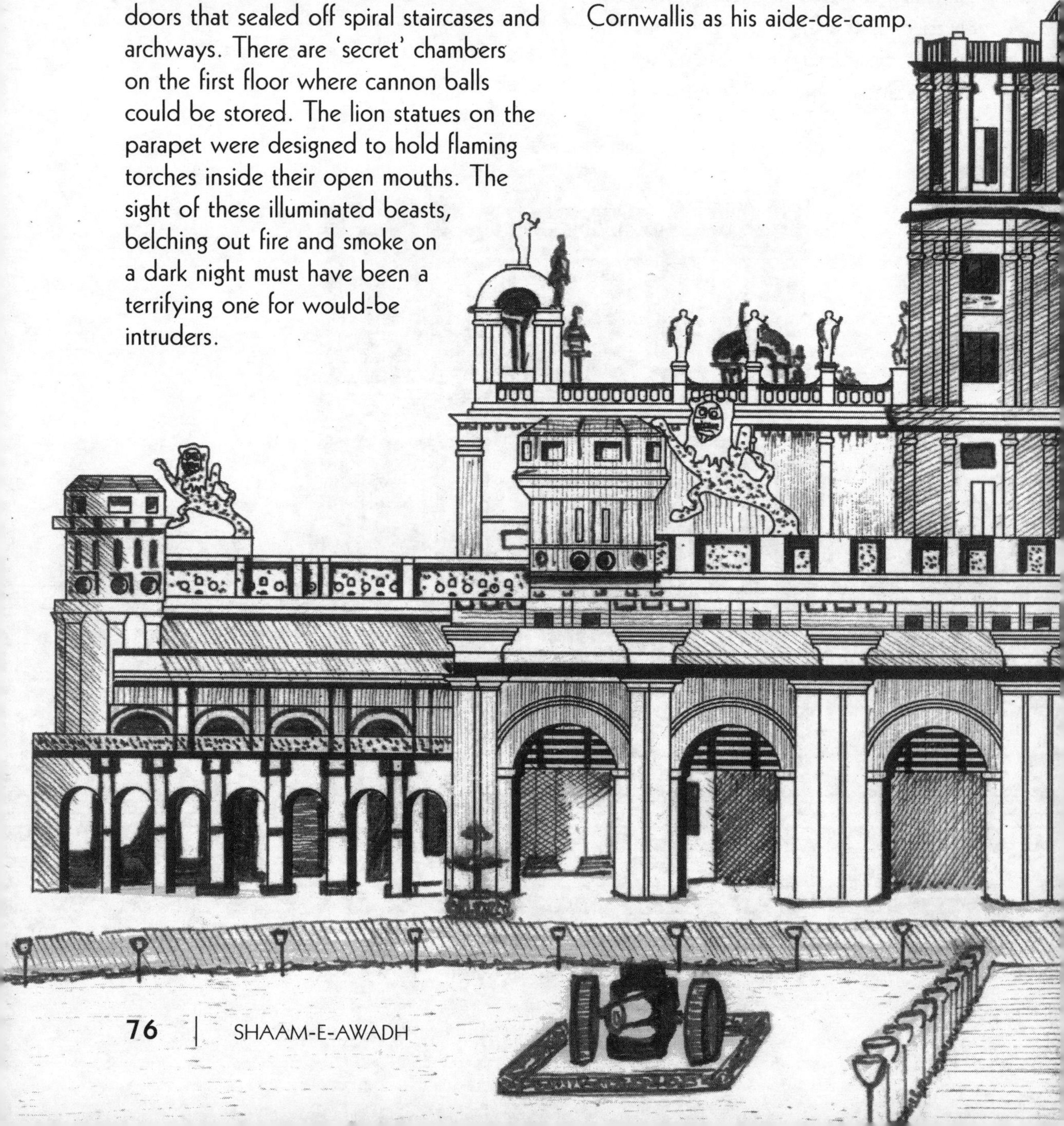

Every visitor of the early 19th century has described these statues on the parapet as: 'Chinese mandarins and ladies with shaking heads and all the gods and goddesses of the heathen mythology', and 'milk maids, shepherdesses, nuns, etc.'

The interior of this building is no less sophisticated than the typical Lucknowite 'Deewankhana'. Its walls and ceiling have beautifully coloured floral designs in 'Meena'. In the central hall there is a portrait of Christ made with coloured glass in the tradition of the Roman Catholic Church. In a circular room, a bust of Martin is kept. The rooms of this palace show a unique collection of oil paintings, medals, trophies and chandeliers.

PINNACLE OF CHHATAR MANZIL

Also known as the Farhat Baksh complex, this Nawabi palace complex was completed by Ghaziud-Din Haidar (4.1814-1827). It consisted of the Greater and Lesser Chhatar Manzils, the Kothi Farhat Bakhsh built by Claude Martin, the Lal Baradari, Gulistan-i-Iram and Darshan Vilas. The complex comprised a sequence of European houses with a central garden and smaller buildings like baradaris and pavilions, covered passageways, gateways and walled area. Ghaziud-Din Haidar completed the unfinished palace on the right bank of the Gomti, near Kothi Farhat Bakhsh. It was earlier built by Nawab Saadat Ali Khan in memory of his mother, Chhatar Kunwar. The palace was crowned by a golden pinnacle in the form of an umbrella.

This pinnacle became so popular that almost all the later domed buildings were decorated with an umbrella in the form of the crown of Awadh, particularly Kothi Kaisar Bagh, Kaisar Pasand and Lakhi Darwaza. The river Gomti and the Khas Bazar formed the northern and southern edges of the compound.

LAKHI GATES OF THE MAGNIFICENT KAISARBAGH PALACE

As soon as Wajid Ali Shah ascended the throne in 1847, he began the construction of the Kaisarbagh palace. Known as an acclaimed singer and a poet rather than a good administrator Wajid Ali Shah visualised a palace complex that amalgamated all the intricacies of a paradise garden.

At the heart of the palace complex was placed the main quadrangle, which had an elaborate charbagh. Through two identical gates known as Lakhi gates, the palace could be entered. It was known as the 'Paree (Angel) Khana' where the queens of the King lived and it is this part that remains intact today.

The two Lakhi gates are today but a shadow of their magnificent past. From dominating the entry into the palace complex, they appear humbled by the volume of traffic rumbling under their aged portals.

LUCKNOW KI MACHHLIYA

Lucknow is a city of magnificent and ornate gateways. While touring around the city, one is sure to pass through one of these beautiful 'Darwazas'. Welcoming the visitors on every gate of the city is a pair of fish. The tale of these two fishes, that form the leitmotif of Awadhi culture in the architectural marvels and decorative art, is intriguing, and is wrapped under several layers of history and mystery.

The origin of these fish is definitely the 'Maahi-Maratib', a Mughal military honour with its roots in Persia. It was bestowed by the Mughals on their exemplary military commanders. Historians are divided on how it reached Lucknow. Maahi-Maratib used to be a fierce looking head of a fish mounted on a staff. This was carried in war behind the recipient king or commander. How it came to be a pair of fish instead of just a single fish head can possibly be attributed to a popular story of Nawab Saadat Khan Burhan-ul-Mulk. It is said that after being appointed the Governor of Awadh, on his way to Lucknow from Farukkhabad, he was crossing the river Ganga and two fish leaped into his lap. This was considered a good omen. The two fish, symbolizing good luck reached Lucknow along with Nawab Saadat Khan and thus began the golden era of the history of Awadh.

THE LUCKYCHARM MERMAIDS ALLOVER...

Every ruler and habitué of Lucknow, native or foreign, has contributed, in greater or lesser measure, to the architectural skyline of the city. The resultant heterogeneity of cultural conceptions and artistic styles could have spelled architectural anarchy for Lucknow. The triumph of harmony and balance in the buildings of Lucknow despite the diverse influences to which their builders were subject, is a tribute to its evolved aesthetic sense.

THE EXOTIC KATHAK – ITS ORIGIN

Among the descendants of the Brahmin Kathaks, Thakur Prasad and Durga Prasad became the respected dance-gurus of Nawab Wajid Ali Shah. In the Mughal court, Persian costumes, romantic themes and Persian names such as aanad, salaami peshkaar and nikaas were introduced. Lucknowi Kathak as it exists today is the result of the combined genius and creativity of the Kalka Binda brothers. Their family residence in Lucknow, Kalka-Binda-ki-deorhi, is the real birthplace of pilgrimage for Kathak lovers, students and scholars. When the two brothers were alive, it was the meeting–place of great artistes from all over north India and the deorhi constantly throbbed with musical sounds, percussion rhythms and the tinkling of hundreds of ghungroos. The family tradition was continued by the triumvirate: Achhan Maharaj excelled in chaals and lightning footwork, Lachhu Maharaj enriched the graceful laasya aspect while Shambhoo Maharaj became famous as the Abhinaya Samrat of Kathak.

CONTRIBUTION OF LUCKNOW TO THE MUSIC WORLD

Lucknow has contributed music directors, (Naushad, Madan Mohan, Roshan), actors and actresses (Kumar, Iftekar, Akhtari Bai, Bina Rai, Yashodhara Katju, Swaranlata), singers (Talat Mahmood, Anup Jalota, Dilraj Kaur, Krishna Kalle), writers (Amritlal Nagar, Bhagawati Sharan Varma, Achala Nagar), lyricists and dancers. Lachhu Maharaj was a very successful choreographer for many films. Pahadi Sanyal, Leela Desai and Kamlesh Kumari of New Theatres at Calcutta were all trained here. However, the musician who gave a distinct stamp of her own to Lucknowi thumri and ghazal was Begum Akhtar.

KANKAVE BAAZI

That is exactly what kite means in Lucknow. A wondrous pastime – some times full-time too! Not only kids but Bade Miyans (as an elderly person is respectfully referred to in Lucknow) too take to rooftops, banks of the river Gomti, embankments, pavements and sometimes even roads where traffic has to wait till the flyers finish with their oh-so-important task of flying kites, cutting another kite or grabbing the falling ones. All this and more is a usual scene in the old city of Lucknow.

THE MESMERIZING KITES

It comes not from the pen of a professional writer of travel books but from the diary of one of the world's first war correspondents – Sir William Russell, correspondent of LondonTimes. He was sent to India to cover the campaign of Sir Colin Campbell, the British Commander-in-Chief, entrusted with the suppression of the Indian Mutiny, otherwise called the first war of Independence.

He further wrote, "Sun playing on all the gilt domes and spires, the exceeding richness of the vegetation and forests and gardens which remind one somewhat of the view of the Bois de Boleyn from the hill over St. Cloud but for the thunder of the guns and the noise of balls clearing the air, how peaceful the scene is! Up above the gilded spires of Kaiserbagh are to be seen many kites serenely floating in the air and giving infinite pleasure to the gentlemen who are directing their movements."He was standing,spellbound, on the rooftop of Dilkusha palace when he wrote this.

RENAISSANCE OF CUISINE

According to Ibn Battuta, the famous Moroccan traveller, kebabs were served in the royal houses as early as 1200 AD, when not only the royal households but commoners too enjoyed a breakfast of kebab and naan.

It is said that when Alexander the Great met King Porus, he was, to his surprise, offered meat mish-mashes that were similar to kebabs of Greece. But the official entry of kebabs into India, and to Oudh (Awadh) region, is credited to Sadat Ali Khan, Burhan ul Mulk, the first Nawab of Oudh from Persia. Albeit then the kebabs were a mere shadow of what they eventually became.

By the time Nawab Asafuddaula came to power, the British had taken over the complete reigns of the kingdom, leaving him to concentrate on what he considered to be his life's two big ambitions: building architectural masterpieces and evolving Awadhi cuisine. Dishes like parind puri (a live bird inside a poori), patili kebab, moti pulao and the arvi ka salan were invented during this period, which culinary historians often refer to as the 'Renaissance of Cuisine'. Innovation became the key to survival for rakabdar as they devised newer ways of slow cooking, smoke flavouring and of course using exotic ingredients like sandalwood, juniper berries, rosebuds, rose, red gensing, to outdo each other every time.

PAAN AND ITS LOVERS

"Qayamat khez hai surkhi yeh paanon ki lab-e tar mein,
Khuda jaane yeh dono laal hain kis ke muqaddar mein"

As rightly mentioned by Abdul Halim Sharar in his legendary book 'Guzishta Lucknow'; it was at the court of Lucknow, above all others that the late Mughal civilisation reached the zenith of its splendour and sophistication. The high culture of Lucknow which was flowering from the 18th century until today can be seen in various art forms present in the city. Paandaan, Khaasdaan and Ughaldaan display the perfect picture of 'Lucknawi Ethnicity'. The idea of 'paandaan' or betel box which turns raw betel leaf into a thing of glory called 'paan' is one of a kind.The idea of paandaan was brought to Lucknow from Delhi, and modifications were made here which are followed till date.

THE INTIMATE AMBIENT MEHFILS

Only Wajid Ali Shah in his moment of intense grief could say poignant verses like:

"Babul mora naihar chhuto hi jaaye,chaar kahaar mill mori doliyan utthave..."

Today, we have many acoustically superior and comfortable auditoria all over the city, but the mehfils of the past had a certain intimate atmosphere which is missing in these halls. But when Ustad Faiyaz Khan sang these lines in his vibrant rich voice with greatdepth of feeling he brought tears to thousand of eyes.

Lucknow offered lavish patronage and lavish darbars to decaying Delhi's music, dance and poetry. Therefore it is rightfully said 'Jab Delhi ujadi, Lucknow bani'. Still, this culture of mehfils at home, patronizing local creativity and talent is prevalent in the city's ethos.

THE FLOURISHING QAWWALI OF AWADH

Lucknow Gharana of Qawwali singing started with the famous Qawwal named Ghulam Rasool, who was influenced by Amir Khusro. Some of the followers migrated to Gwalior, like, Bade Mohammad Khan and Naththan Peerbux and created this new Gharana. 'Tappa', another form was invented by Shori Miyan, a descendent of Ghulam Rasool.

AN INCREDIBLE CITY

It has been a long journey, but that has not subdued the aroma of Awadhi delicacies. Tundey kebabs continue to tickle the taste buds of celebrities and commoners alike. Be it Raja's thandai, Netram's lassi, Ram Asrey's malai paan or Chowk's makkhan malai, they all have retained the old flavour. So has Lucknow's chaat, a fact certified by visitors, though its style of presentation has changed a lot. Over the years, there have been new additions too in the street food – momos and vegetable kebabs for instance. Amid the uncountable roadside stalls, Sharma's chai and Bajpai's poori still perk up the olfactory buds of Lucknowallahs.

Incidentally, the first successful iteration of the galwati kebab had all the above-mentioned ingredients along with real pearl and gold and some guarded aphrodisiacs, which was suggested by the hakim in an attempt to egg the Nawab to do some activity. Did it have the famed 160 spices? With no records available, there is no way of finding out, but surviving khansamas believe it wasn't the case.

TUNDAY KABABI

The story goes that by then the Nawab, who was an infamous couch potato, had lost the use of his dentures and was looking for something pate style, which needed no chewing yet imparted the flavours of a fine kebab.

Finally, it was Haji Murad Ali, one of the finest chefs of the time, who got the consistency right. It is said that Ali, who was working on perfecting the mixture of the shahi galawat, fell off the roof and broke his arm. But the injury didn't stop him from working on the kebab. After, some say, a year and a half, Ali discovered what his one arm could do – pound the meat dough into such fine paste that it would melt in your mouth, and would take on the clove dum really well.

FILMS ON LUCKNOW

A famous scene from Ray's film depicts Wajid Ali Shah leisurely playing chess as the British soldiers march in. But these much-maligned Nawabs were responsible for nurturing Lucknow's culture of poetry, dance, music and art and inventing the famous Lucknowi traditions.

No other city in India, except Kolkata, has inspired so much research, with innumerable books having been written on it. With its colonial roots and its role as a catalyst of the freedom movement, the city has and will continue to spawn research. The presence of archives also helps. Others like photographer John Paulo, for example, or filmmakers and TV crews from the national and international media come armed with just curiosity, seeking traces of a lost era that they have heard, read or been inspired by. It's worth taking a look at the movies which have had Lucknow as their backdrop – 'Shatranj Ke Khiladi, Mere Mehboob, Palki, Chaudhavin Ka Chand, Pakeeza, Junoonand Umrao Jaan' are just a few of them.

OUTCOME OF FIRST WAR OF INDEPENDENCE

The Residency complex today consists of ruins of several buildings; each ruin has its own story to tell about the events of 1857. The buildings were usually named after the persons who lived there. These are still there like Dr. Fayerer's house, Brigade mets, Sago's House, Kanpur Battery, Redan Battery, Sikh Square, Anderson's Post, etc., and the area covered was about 33 acres. It also has a museum which contains beautiful and very old photos of ancient Lucknow and its monuments. There is also a Tahkhana (dungeon, basement) inside the building, from where a spiraling set of 44 stairs go down.

THE RESIDENCY

The Lucknow Residency is the centrepiece of one of the most dramatic sieges of all time. To commemorate the gallantry of both besieged and besiegers, the Government of India has, through its Archaeological Survey Department, kept the Residency in exactly that state to which it was reduced by the end of the five-month siege. What remains today is but a fraction of the original 28 buildings and batteries – only six are reasonably intact – Dr. Fayrer's House, the Main Residency Building, the Banqueting Hall, The Treasury, Bailey Guard Gate and Begum Kothi. A few, like, Martiniere Post and Anderson's Post, Germon's Post, Sikh Square and Horses Square are a little more than a few crumbling walls and foundations. The rest have vanished. The smouldering resentment burst into the flame of open rebellion on May 30, 1857, in the cantonments at Muriaon, to the north of the Gomti river. Bungalows were burnt and attempts made on the lives of British officers...some were killed. Soon there was nothing to do, from the British point of view, but to withdraw to as safe a place as possible, and defy the rising tide of rebellion.

Surrounded thus by thousands of enemies, the British and their allies, under the leadership of the Chief Commissioner of Awadh, Sir Henry Lawrence, withdrew to the Residency complex and to the Machhi Bhawan. The first relief operation took place on September 25, 1857 when General Havelock's little column of fewer than 1,000 men fought their way into the Residency, with very heavy losses.

It was on 17 November 1857 that Sir Colin Campbell entered the Residency and two days later marched out to freedom. The British had suffered severe losses, and most of Lucknow was in the hands of Hazrat Mahal, Begum of Awadh. Sir Henry Lawrence was buried in the Residency grounds and his wishes were followed, as can be seen by the visitor. Strangely, his death was as much mourned by his enemies as his friends, for he was a good and kind man, and had in his career done a lot to improve the lot of the poor. Diseases, like smallpox, but especially cholera, took a heavy toll, particularly as rations were cut, and medicines ran short.

The climax came on June 30. Report came in to Sir Henry that a force of rebels was moving in on Lucknow to attack the British. They met at Chinhat and the British were soundly beaten by a force of some 5,000 well-armed and well-led men. What was left of the British force retreated painfully back over the Iron Bridge and straggled into the Residency, to have its wounds attended to. An uneasy calm descended on the place. The siege of the Lucknow Residency had begun.

THE PEACE OF METHODIST CHURCH

It was built in 1877 although the congregation of this church had started worships in 1870. The first Indian pastor (priest) of this church was Rev. William Jeffroy who served here from 1940 to 1944. It is a beautiful and well-maintained church.

It may be the land where a Nawab's mysterious death in the hidden ante chambers of Kothi Gulistane-Iram occupies coffeetable conversations, but it is also a city where the country's foreign policy is debated hotly. The world may quote Mirza Ghalib's unforgettable couplets, but it is Lucknow that can stake claim to his rich legacy with Majaz's shayari.

Lucknow is an incredible city, no doubt, but now it has an odd arrangement of buildings wherein the new and tall ones are pushing hard to squeeze into spaces sheltering old heritage buildings and monuments.

Grandeur of Charbagh & chessboard

It incorporates the mix of Rajput, Awadhi and Mughal architecture;Charbagh Station, the major railway station of Lucknow, is an architectural masterpiece. The structural design of Charbagh Railway Station enthralls a tourist at the onset. Built at a whopping price of Rs. 70 lakhs, it was designed by J.H. Hornimen. The foundation of the Charbagh Railway Station was laid by the Bishop in March 1914. On April 23, 1867, the 47-mile Lucknow-Kanpur section was opened for traffic. This became part of the Oudh Rohilkhand Railway. The present Lucknow division, was part of East Indian Railway from 1912 to 1952.

One hardly becomes aware of the sound and commotion accompanying the arrival and departure of trains. Incidentally while the first aspect symbolizes a traditional sport of Nawabi era, the other is representative of Lucknow's 'Tehzeeb'. In the beauty of its architectural composition, the Charbagh railway station has no parallel in this country except Mumbai Railway Station and is perhaps one of the most attractive railway stations in the world.

Foundation of Charbagh was laid in the area north of Munavar Bagh of Lucknow. With the decline of Nawab's rule, the garden too lost its importance due to prolonged neglect. The rail link to Lucknow was through the Aishbagh railway station. The land of Charbagh railway station complex was acquired after allotment of Purani Imli of Maulviganj to the nawabs of Char Mahal and Charbagh in lieu of the above property. The blueprint for this grandiose building was prepared by the famous architect Sir Swinton Jacob.

Lucknow's Charbagh Railway Station, till 1867, was a large orchard. The present Station building was constructed in 1926 with domes and minars of Indo-Sarcenicdesign, intended to harmonise with the architecture peculiar to the important historical buildings of the city which date to the days of the Nawabs of Oudh. The Rajput architecture in red and white gives it a stately appearance. Besides, in two aspects it is different from any other building of this country. In an aerial view, the station building with its big and small domes appears as a chessboard laid with pieces. The second interesting aspect of this building is its acoustics which is soundproof.

THE ESSENCE OF DUSSEHRI MANGOES

The fresh Dussehri mango is a very juicy and sweet fruit with a unique and delicious taste. The Kakori Dussehri is, indeed, highly rated for its looks, colour, smell and taste.

Legend has it that a Pathan of Khalispur village of Malihabad tehsil transporting choicest mangoes for trade happened to halt for rest in a hut of a poor Momedian, a monk. Momedian patronized travellers by offering water and shelter and the travellers reciprocated with ripe mangoes. At the time of departure, the Pathan and the monk had an argument. In a fit of rage, the Pathan shoved one of his choicest ripe mangoes into the soil instead of gifting it to the monk, who maintained utmost calm and restraint. In the ensuing rainy season, a mango sapling from the spot emerged which was duly nurtured to a robust tree by Momedian. After about 12 years, the tree flowered profusely and yielded fruits of excellent quality. The news of this unique mango reached the Nawab who owned the land. He took due care to protect and conserve this exquisite mango variety which later became the popular 'Dussehri' variety of north India.

KING GEORGE MEDICAL COLLEGE – ITS ENVIRONS

Located in Chowk in Lucknow, this medical college is the best Medical Institute of the state. The idea of establishing a medical college was given by King Emperor, George V, and hence the college is named after him. The architecture of the building is designed in Indo-Sarcenic style so that it matches the other buildings of historical importance. Sir Swinton Jacob was the architect of the building.

I had been wandering in the old city, or Chowk, on the Gol Darwaza side where Raja Thandai is. He offers a milk drink aptly called thandai infused with saffron, khus syrup (the cool grass-like scent, syruped), or bhang, which underscores the reason why a blue poison blooded Shiva Shankar sits auspiciously at the back. There were dishes displaying beauty, wealth and subtlety such as the Moti Pullao where the silver and gold leaf are mixed with rawa and stuffed into the neck of the chicken and then wound with string, or of exoticism and uniqueness such as a roghan josh called Aloo ki Bukhara, meaning small dried Bukharan plums, never seen in the dish.

THE CHANGING SOCIETY...

The historic Asafi Imambara mosque in Lucknow is rewriting tradition.
A small 'revolutionary' step has been taken by a group of young Shia women – offering 'namaz' at the mosque.
Yet several others are being encouraged to follow suit. A burqa-clad lady, who runs a boutique in the heart of the city, is among those who plan to make a beginning during the Ramzan month.

THE NEW LABYRINTH OF STREETS

In the aftermath of 1857 both the physical form and the social organization of the city underwent a dramatic change. The entire area surrounding the major historical precincts along the river was cleared of all habitation seen as a threat to the Residency, leaving a vast tract of open space. For similar 'security' reasons, further to the south, the authorities cut straight, wide roads across the fabric of the city, where previously there was a maze of streets and lanes.

Also, as part of the measures following 1857, large parts of the Kaiserbagh palace complex were demolished, and the buildings spared were either appropriated by the British for their own use with modifications or granted to "friendly natives". The latter included several of the Taluqdars of Awadh, who had been by and large loyal to the British. They were allowed to build their own houses on the fringes of the Kaiserbagh complex.

The period from 1857 to 1947 also witnessed the building of a number of palatial residences for high-ranking functionaries of the Empire, the adaptive reuse of some old secular buildings, and the construction of new buildings in composite architectural style superimposing traditional exteriors on modern functions.

IN TRANSITION…

The ordinary Muslim, who is neither a Nawab, nor a terrorist, nor a fundamentalist, sometimes tends to get overlooked as if he/she does not exist. Middleclass-ness among Lucknowi Muslims, thus, has proved to be an extremely contested cultural project within a field of competing discourses and corresponding aspirations, consumption markers, and lifestyles.

Not particularly concerned with the simultaneity of politicization of religious identities, the media-based commercialization of religion, an increasing ritualization of religious practice, a celebrated pro-science and technology approach, and the compulsions of globalization of consumption culture have made the Muslim middle class, as one student of the Lucknow University summed up, 'lost in transition.'

NEW STRIDES – SCIENTIFIC CONVENTION CENTRE

This is a grand structure built on the Sardar Patel Hostel grounds at one end of Shahmina Road. The centre has been taken over by King George Medical University and is used for national and international scientific and cultural functions of the university and other bodies as well. The centre has state-of-the-art audio-visual facilities. The auditoria can be used for plays, music as well as films. It is in harmony with the grandeur of the skyline.

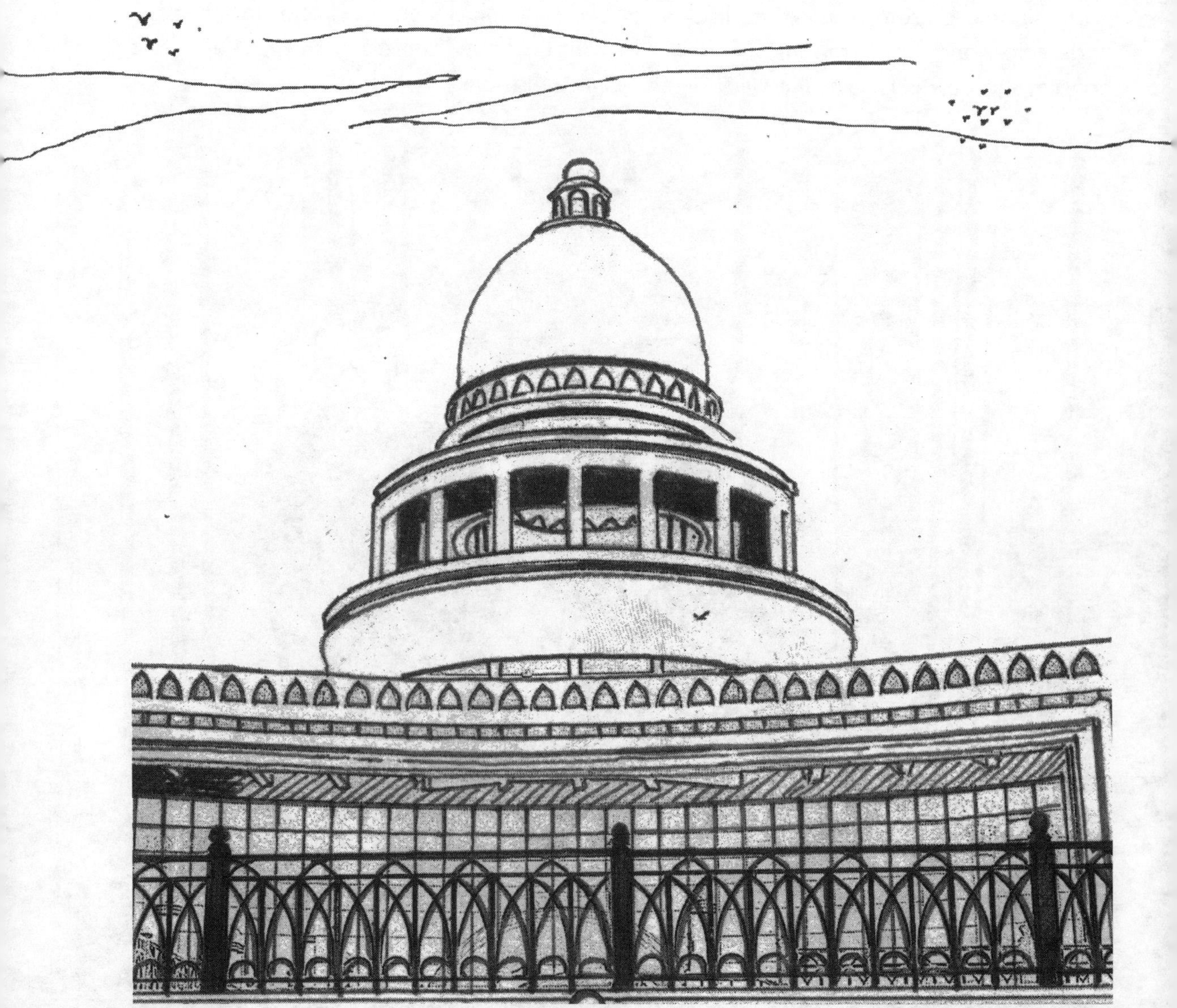

THE EFFECTS OF GLOBALISATION

The erosion of the essential culture of the city calling it a bigger crime than the erosion of much of its architectural heritage. One follows the other and it leaves the city stripped of its character in the bargain, she says. People have learnt to accept that modern demands are taking their toll on the Nawabi city and that graciousness and spaciousness will be things of the past if attempts are not made to preserve the pockets in which they remain today.

EROSION… IN THE CONTEXT OF LUCKNOW

Estimates of the number of slums in Lucknow vary. Certainly, the areas of poor housing are found on the fringes of the city, on the banks of the river, arid nallahs near railway tracks, as well as other areas. These slums are sometimes in large well-defined settlements, but often in scattered clusters in the interstices between better housing. There is a huge disparity between the level of service prevailing in planned settlements and unorganized slum clusters; this leads to both social discontent and frustration among the poor.

JOURNEY DOWN THE RIVER

Many urban spaces in Lucknow are also memorial sites either because they contain heritage structures or they are designated or designed as memorial parks and plazas with graves, obelisks, canopies, gateways, and statuary. They are the epitome of architectural excellence, markers of momentous events in urban history, and reminders of contributions made by individuals towards the greater public good. While buildings, memorial tablets and plaques, and other building elements constitute the former two groups, commemoration of great personages occurs exclusively through iconography. The riverfront provides an opportunity to reclaim derelict space for civic purposes including memorials. The journey down the river could be an encounter with historic Lucknow.

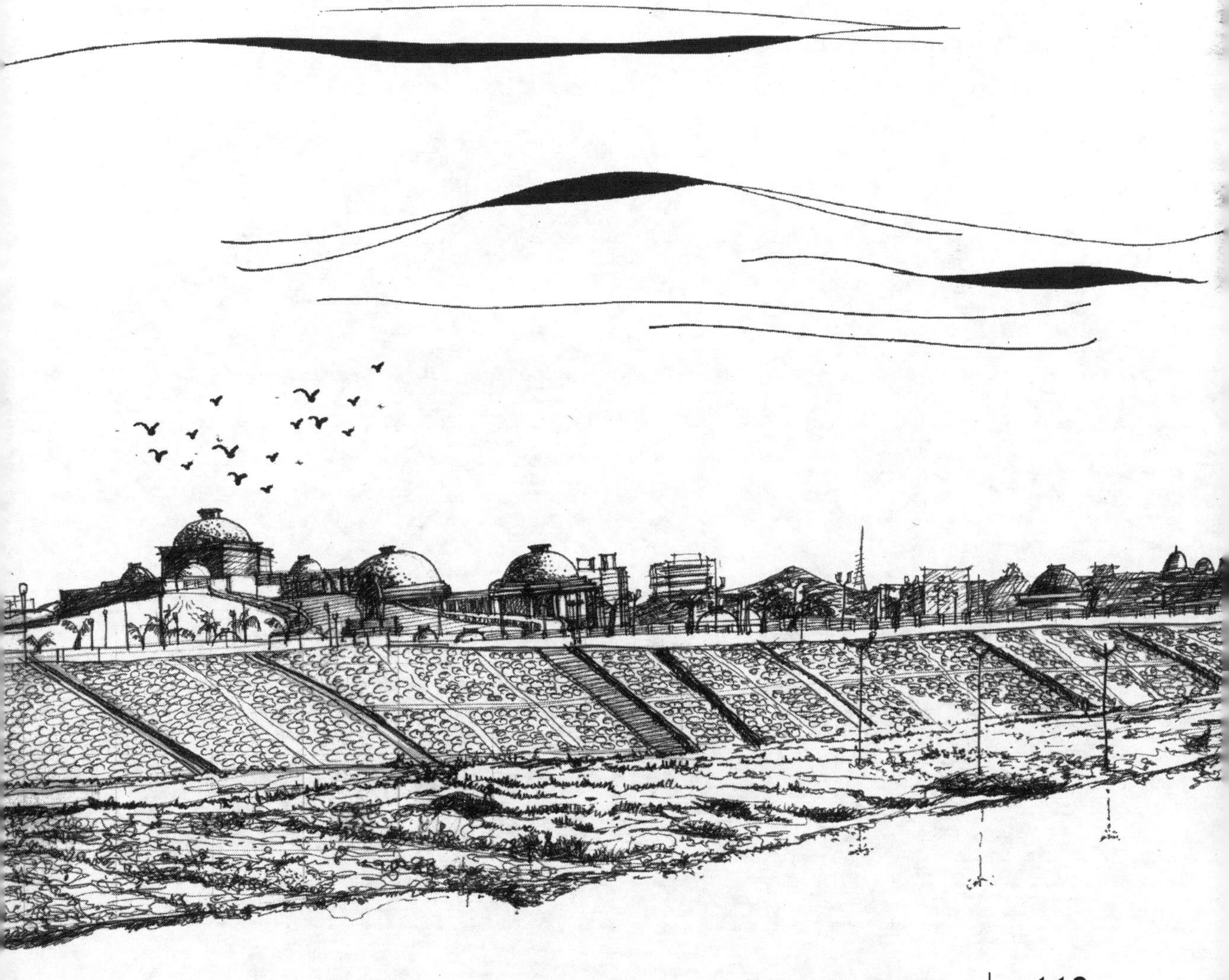

THE NEW URBAN SPACES

The Ambedkar Udyan, renamed as Ambedkar Samajik Parivartan Sthal or Site of Social Change, on the banks of the river Gomti, has become a major landmark of Lucknow. Sprawling over 25acres, the domed memorial hall crowns a cascading structure 112ft high above the road level, visible from miles around. Replete with Buddhist imagery – Chaitya openings, domes reminiscent of stupas, elephants – the form is derivative of the Indic archetype of the sacred hill ringed by the seven seas. The landscape design is based on the mandala pattern – square set within a circle and ringed by lotus petals. The eight principles of Buddhism are symbolized in the eight sections of the landscape created by swirling pathways. Cardinal orientation is achieved by entries in four directions, flanked by ramps and steps. Chattries on the elevated terrace provide outlook points to the larger urban landscape of the river Gomti, the street bridge with its gateway over the river, and the riverfront plazas.

THE LUCKNOW IN CHANGE…

"Lucknow was the Baghdad & Cordova of India and Nishapur and Bokhara of the east," writes Abdul Halim Sharar. The heart of this enthralling magnificent city, undoubtedly, lies in this amalgamation of styles.

The courtyard style houses or kothis of mohallas are giving way to eclectic bungalows of Gomtinagar and swanky flyovers and malls. Lucknow is a city once more in transition blessed with a splendid past but, shall be in the years ahead, confronted with great pressures on its historic fabric, which is thirsty for its rejuvenation and conservation.

THE NOVEL MEMORIALS

A library, museum and an administration building to the south and a guesthouse to the east of the Memorial extends the complex to over 60 acres. A raised entry plaza gives a vantage point to the long vista of the Memorial. A steel obelisk slices the Ambedkar Memorial dome and is the central marker in a piazza ringed by the buildings in the south and an amphitheatre in the north.

The buildings, clad in the Dholpur sandstone with glass facades towards the piazza, reflect the Memorial, but fail to achieve the superb harmony of its form in their own design. A four-faced marble statue of Gautam Buddha dominates the soaring skylit three-storey atrium of the Museum and Buddhist urns on pillars line the buildings and form the converging view to the piazza.

Statuary animates the open spaces within the complex and its approach. Two groups of statues of Bhimrao Ambedkar and his wife Ramabai and Mayawati and Kanshi Ram line the main entry to the complex. The riverfront plaza has Ramabai Ambedkar's statue and upon entering the complex, one is greeted with Dr. Ambedkar's statues in his characteristic pose. The foursome of Parivartan Chowk – Jyotirao Phule, Narayan Guru, Shahuji Maharaj and Bhimrao Ambedkar – tower over the raised plaza at the entry to the Samajik Parivartan Library and Museum. Elephants, the party symbol, add to the iconography.

The term 'sthal', sacred symbols such as the 'yantra' and 'mandala' patterns in design, and deification of historic and contemporary figures suggest a sacred site and this is what declared the complex to be a place of pilgrimage.

THE MARINE DRIVE OF LUCKNOW

The Marine Drive, a magnificent and spectacular strip along the Gomti river, is impressive. It is a favourite hangout zone for the younger lot. In the evening, one can see many locals and tourists strolling along the place.

The cold breeze, the mesmerising scenic beauty is beyond doubt catching up as a favoured zone. The pathways have garden benches for visitors to just sit, relax and enjoy the beauty.

The sunset at Marine Drive brings out the exceptional scenic splendour of this place. The 18-feet-high four-faced Buddha statue made of white marble is ornate in the truest sense. The statues here are almost lifelike, such is the detailing. The sprawling lush green gardens appeal to sore eyes, a much-awaited reprieve from the concrete jungles we live in. The banks of the river are beautified and lined with aesthetically placed garden benches.

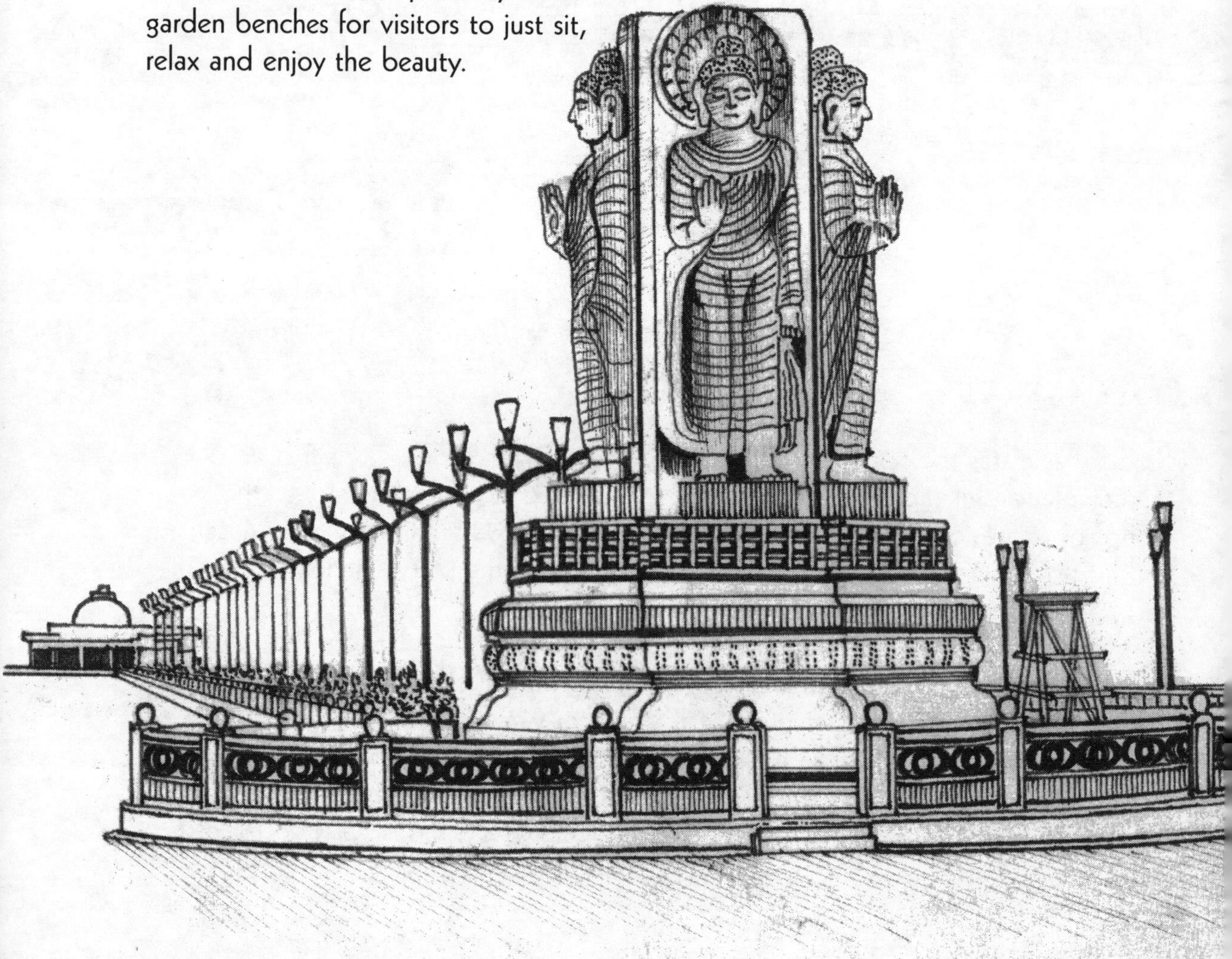

PAAN CHEWING – A CURSE OR ETHNICITY?

Mohammad Ali Shah is credited with having built a Babylon in Lucknow – let's see how long it will take the present generation to preserve one of the finest specimens of that era from crumbling down.

To prepare a perfect paan, one needs to practice under an expert of the art. Paan is not just a betel leaf that is enveloped with requisite ingredients and eaten. The paan leaf stuffed with areca nut (dalli), catechu (Kattha), quick lime (choona), and cardamom (Elaichi) is known as the Plain Paan (Saada Paan). Besides these main ingredients, it may also contain peppermint, qimaam, coconut, misri (crystallized sugar), rose syrup, saffron, sweetened areca nut (sweet and scented supari), and cherry making it the most preferred sweet, flavoured paan.

The paan is then folded in a conical shape known as 'Gilouri' and is also covered with silver foil (chaandikawarq) to make it look more appealing. A clove is used to staple the paan so as to prevent unfolding of the leaf. As paan chewing is a culture in Lucknow, its processing also entails skill and practice as adding all the ingredients in the right amount is the trick to preparing the right paan.

SITE OF SOCIAL CHANGE

Parivartan Chowk, north of Kaiserbagh and east of Begum Hazrat Mahal Park, is an urban insertion made in 1995. A rather tall vertical structure holding a globe at its summit and sheltering a seated statue of the Buddha marks the centre of a huge plaza that acts as a traffic roundabout in the heart of Lucknow.

Four statues of Ambedkar, Phule, Shahuji and Periyar with inscriptions on pedestals mark the cardinal points in the circular plaza where a number of streets converge. This location not only ensures high visibility and landmark status but also marks the arrival of change in a historic area of the Nawabi and colonial times.

THE MELODY OF LUCKNOW

However, the musician who gave a distinct stamp of her own to Lucknowi thumri and ghazal was Begum Akhtar. She was our last and most vital link with Lucknow's colourful musical past.

Her singing always created visions of the glorious and opulent era when high-class music, Urdu poetry, refined tastes, gracious living, polished manners and polite language in everyday life, had all combined to make Lucknowi culture famous and widely admired. Her training in classical music under renowned ustads, her rich and resonant voice, fecund imagination, romantic temperament and thorough knowledge of Urdu poetry and her rich repertoire of thumris, dadras and ghazals made her the most outstanding exponent of these styles. The artistic blend of poorab and punjabang touches was a distinctive feature of her individualistic style.

SAHARA
Ganj
MARKS & SPENCER

THE RECREATION OF OLD IDENTITIES

The urban landscape of Lucknow has evolved to reflect the ongoing social change and the city's aspirations towards the future. Sometimes, in the process, the past is left behind, forgotten in the accelerated rush towards modernity.

BREATHING SPACES

Janeshwar Park will be one of the biggest parks and the country's first fully solar powered one. The park was modelled with Hyde Park in London as an inspiration. The park boasts the following features – green belt spread across the park, twohuge ponds spread over 38 acres, golfcourse, horseriding trails, lakes, sportscentre, gymnasium, theme park and gondola rides.

The sprawling park, spread over 376 acres in Gomti Nagar Extension, has been developed at a cost of Rs 170 crores. The park has a huge lake and water body at the centre spread over 40-45 acres.

Its hydrological and geological plan has been prepared by IIT-Kanpur. The architectural and developmental blueprint has been drafted by the prestigious New Delhi-based School of Planning and Architecture.

We are creating a whole new generation of youth which has still to come to terms with the transition the city is going through. While a sudden influx of money opens vistas and facilitates city life, it also brings with it an apathetic outlook towards the culture that was so cherished once.

THE GONDOLAS OF LUCKNOW

The park boasts of a lake with gondolas. The gondola is a traditional, flat-bottomed Venetian rowing boat, wellsuited to the conditions of the lagoon and now for the lake of the Janeshwar Park. The historical gondola was quite different from its modern evolution; the paintings of Canaletto and others show a much lower prow, a higher ferro, and usually two rowers. The banana-shaped modern gondola was developed only in the 19th century by the boat-builder Tramontin.

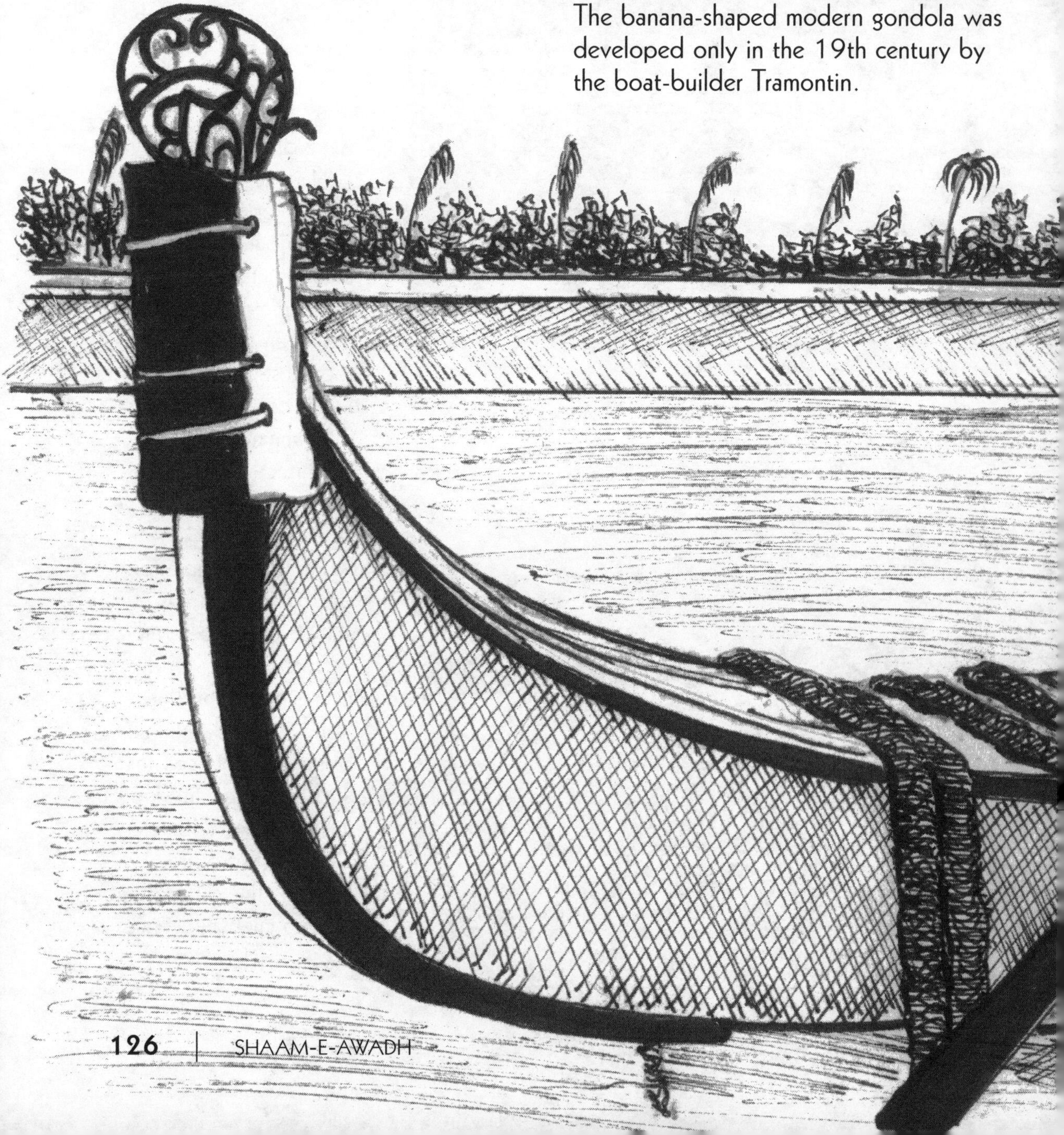

Every detail of the gondola has its own symbolism. The iron prow-head of the gondola, called 'fero da prorà'or 'dol fin',is needed to balance the weight of the gondolier at the stern and has an S shape symbolic of the twists in the Canal Grande. The curved top signifies the Doge's cap. The semicircular break between the curved top and the six teeth is said to represent the Rialto Bridge.

COMMUNAL PEACE AND HARMONY

Lucknow is a model for communal peace in India. Sample this: Lucknow did not erupt when 30,000 refugees came over from West Pakistan after Partition. Nor even when the disputed shrine was demolished in Ayodhya, 70 miles from Lucknow, when the whole country was experiencing the most gruesome riots since Partition. Why are cities like Aligarh, Hyderabad, Ahmedabad, Meerut and Kanpur more riot-prone than Lucknow? The reason is that inter-communal civic life is more prominent in the Nawabi city. Civic links between communities, and not just government initiative, is the biggest guarantor of communal peace.

THE TEMPTATIONS...

Lucknowites seem to be as comfortable with sher-o-shayri and traditional Awadhi cuisine as they are with Shakira's Wherever, Whenever and cappuccino and pasta. Lucknow lives as much in the serpentine bylanes of the Old City as it does in the plush shopping mall of Hazratganj where one can make purchases at the snazziest of showrooms selling international brands of couture and footwear, buy the latest electronics and swankiest cars available in the country.

THE ASPIRATIONS…

Lucknow-Kanpur corridor (90 kms) has some of the greatest land parcels for IT hubs. As the ecosystem influencers come together to channelize this potential, with the right vision and good governance, we can build one of the best tech hubs here. Let's not ignore that Kanpur has an IIT, and Lucknow has an IIM among many other notable institutions.

THE PACE ... THE NEED OF THE HOUR

Victor Hugo once said, "All the forces in the world are not as powerful as an idea whose time has come." Lucknow's time has come. India cannot grow without UP growing.

We have almost one-fifth of India's population and would be the fifth largest nation in terms of population if it were an independent country. We need more of our countrymen to come back from abroad and build Lucknow into a great developed state. There is great talent in Lucknow. Creating opportunities for the talented folks here to stay closer to their homes is of foremost priority.

THE ASSIMILATION…

Though an inheritor of Delhi's architectural tradition, Lucknow's was more than an adaptation. Various regional and local building techniques mingled to give the architecture a distinctive character of its own. However, such perceptions miss the point of this architecture, and discourage others today from engaging with the fascinating forms that emerged from the vibrant interaction of two dynamic cultures.

That such pointed criticism of the buildings persists to the present, relates more to the reliance of current critics upon historic sources, than to the inherent lack of merit or formal sophistication displayed by the buildings themselves.

Little wonder, this uniqueness of the city prompted a poet to comment, "Lucknow hum par fida, hum fida-e Lucknow." Because of its rich cultural heritage and the presence of several historical monuments, Lucknow can surely become a much sought-after destination for tourists.

THE CHARACTER WHICH BECKONS...

The city is famous all over the world for its language, hospitality, sophistication and courteousness. It offers the best of both worlds and is an essential balm for jiggling nerves. Lucknow invariably fascinates whoever visits the city. This city grows on the residents as well as visitors. The city surely has a distinct personality and a character of its own which attracts people like a magnet.

Thus Lucknow developed its own identity not only in architecture but also in the decorative arts, music, poetry, theatre, dress, etiquette, hospitality, cuisine, and a number of other aspects of culture. What is more, Muslims and Hindus alike identified strongly with all these aspects of culture. It was a truly composite culture, and its essential features are recognizable in the city to this day.

Talk with the Author-Artist

'This is a dream publishing project for me', she says. 'I've always loved travelling and taking my sketchbooks with me.

"Lucknow" is very much part of my psyche. Now that I live in Gomtinagar, the new Lucknow but, I really appreciate coming back with fresh eyes each time I take my car to the older parts. With my sketches, I attempt to capture the different textures and tones of the city, depicting both the landmarks and smaller, out-of-the-way sights and museums. It was really important for the book to feel complete, but in a way it's also about sharing my personal take on the city. Each one I've chosen holds memories for me; they have a special significance.'

For each location, she would identify and isolate a key feature. 'It's about communicating information: paring things to their essentials, with a historical significance and trying to get a single picture to convey the atmosphere and some of the detail of the place to the reader.'

Although some of the finer details are added later in her studio, she always sketches on location. 'It really is the only way to get that atmosphere, otherwise there's no feeling, no life behind the illustrations. It's so important to go there and experience the place.' She encourages travelers to use a pencil to capture vacation memories rather than a camera and believes that 'sketching makes for a richer travel experience'. Urban sketching is definitely not as easy as it sounds. Looking at the sketches in the book and reading the tips shared, it is obvious that a great deal of practice and patience is required.

Her favourite thing about Lucknow is 'the sheer diversity of culture, which can almost be quite overwhelming. But if you just delve into it and enjoy it it's just one of the most fascinating cities – it's got so much history and it's evolving constantly.'